COMBAT NURSES
of WORLD WAR II

by Wyatt Blassingame
illustrated by Gil Walker

Purple House Press
Kentucky

To
Kathi Diamant

For permission to quote from books and letters, grateful acknowledgment is made to the following: The John Day Company, Inc., for quotations and letters by Lt. Sally Zumaris in *With Love, Jane* by Alma Lutz (John Day, 1945); Dorothea Daley Engel, Crowell Collier and Macmillan, Inc., for a quotation from "I Was Married in Battle," *American Magazine*, October, 1942; Patricia Lockridge Hartwell, Crowell Collier and Macmillan, Inc., for a quotation from "Solace at Iwo," *Woman's Home Companion*, May, 1945; Leota Hurley Leavens for quotations from a letter; Agnes Jensen Mangerich for quotations from letters; Putnam's and Coward-McCann for a quotation from *Helmets and Lipstick* by Ruth Haskell (G.P. Putnam's Sons, 1944); Simon and Schuster, Inc., for quotations from *Purple Heart Valley* by Margaret Bourke-White (Simon and Schuster, 1944); Al K. Smith for quotations from letters of Phyllis MacDonald Smith; Keith Wheeler and Shirley Collier for a quotation from *We are the Wounded* (E.P. Dutton, 1945).

Photo credit page 4: U.S. Navy

Published by
Purple House Press
PO Box 787
Cynthiana, Kentucky 41031

Classic Books for Kids and Young Adults
purplehousepress.com

Copyright © 1967 by Wyatt Blassingame. Printed with permission from the estate of Wyatt Blassingame
"About the Author" copyright © 2021 by Kathi Diamant
Cover artwork © 2021 by Purple House Press
Revised edition
All rights reserved

ISBN 9781948959476 Hardcover
ISBN 9781948959568 Paperback

CONTENTS

1.	The Beginning	5
2.	Bataan and Corregidor	18
3.	England	35
4.	North Africa	45
5.	Italy	58
6.	Training for War	73
7.	Islands of the Pacific	81
8.	Hospital Ship	92
9.	Flight Nurse	104
10.	France and Germany	119
11.	Prisoners of War	132
	Author's Note	141
	About the Author	142
	Pacific Theater map	6
	European Theater map	37

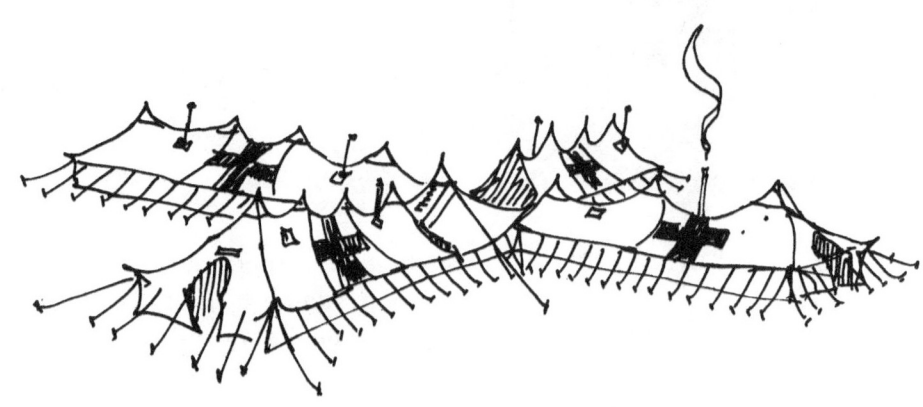

Jane Kendeigh (p. 106-7) was the first naval flight nurse to set foot on an active battlefield. Seen here March 6, 1945, as she was evacuating patients from Iwo Jima. The flight nurses helped evacuate 2,393 Marines and Sailors between March 6-21, 1945. "Candy" continued her nursing career after leaving the Navy.

THE BEGINNING
CHAPTER ONE

It was a Sunday morning, December 7, 1941. In Pearl Harbor, Hawaii, the hospital ship *Solace* lay quietly at anchor. She had been newly converted and her fresh white paint glittered in the early sunlight. Down her white side, from stem to stern, ran a broad green stripe. In the center of this was a huge red cross. Another red cross was painted on the white smokestack. Against the placid water of the harbor the ship looked very peaceful and very pretty.

At five minutes to eight Lieutenant Grace Lally, Chief Nurse on the *Solace*, was in her cabin dressing for church. She could hear airplanes, but this was not surprising. Both the army and navy had airfields nearby and planes were always passing overhead. Even when Miss Lally heard the sound of guns she thought only that it was another drill—

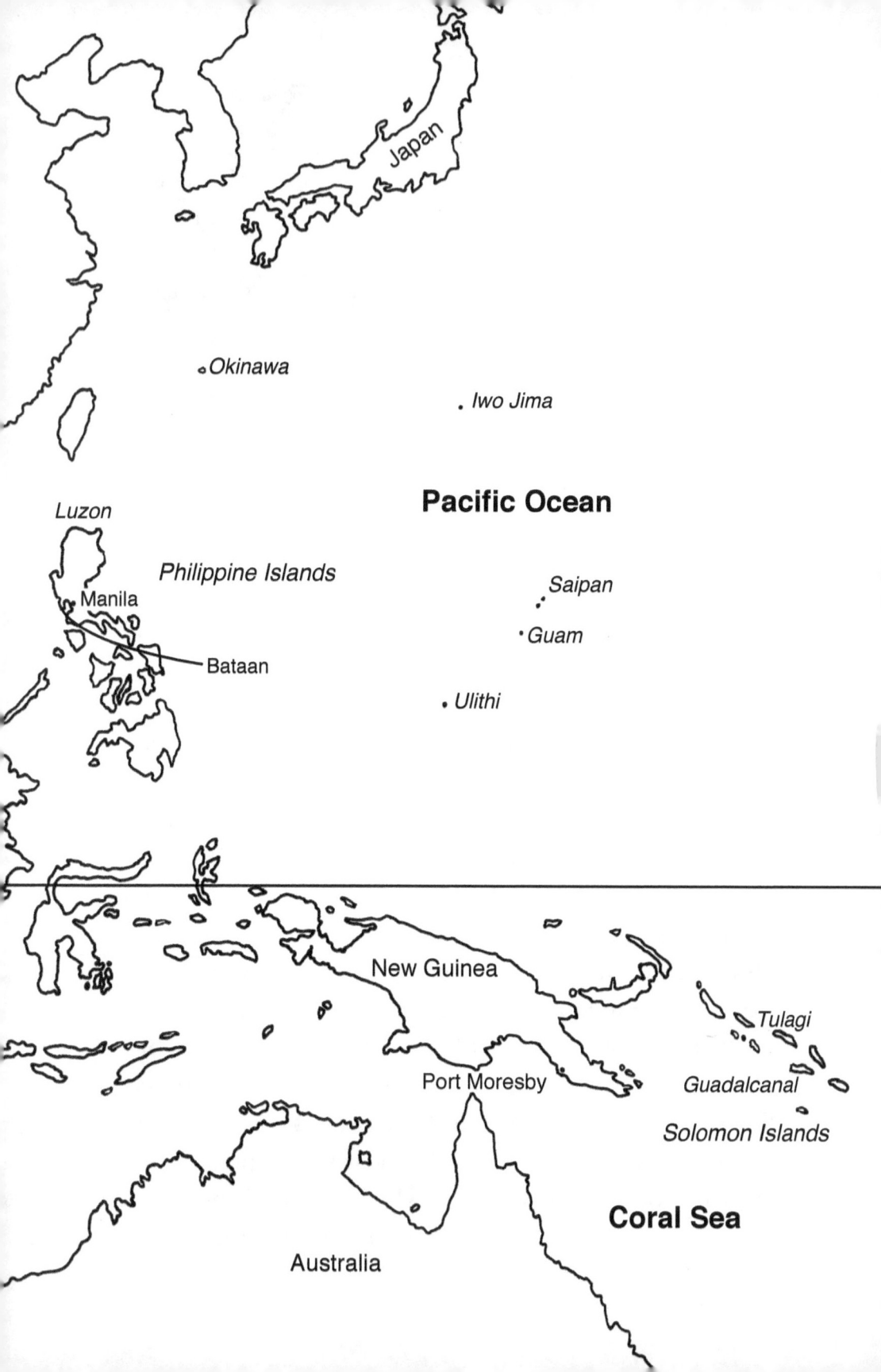

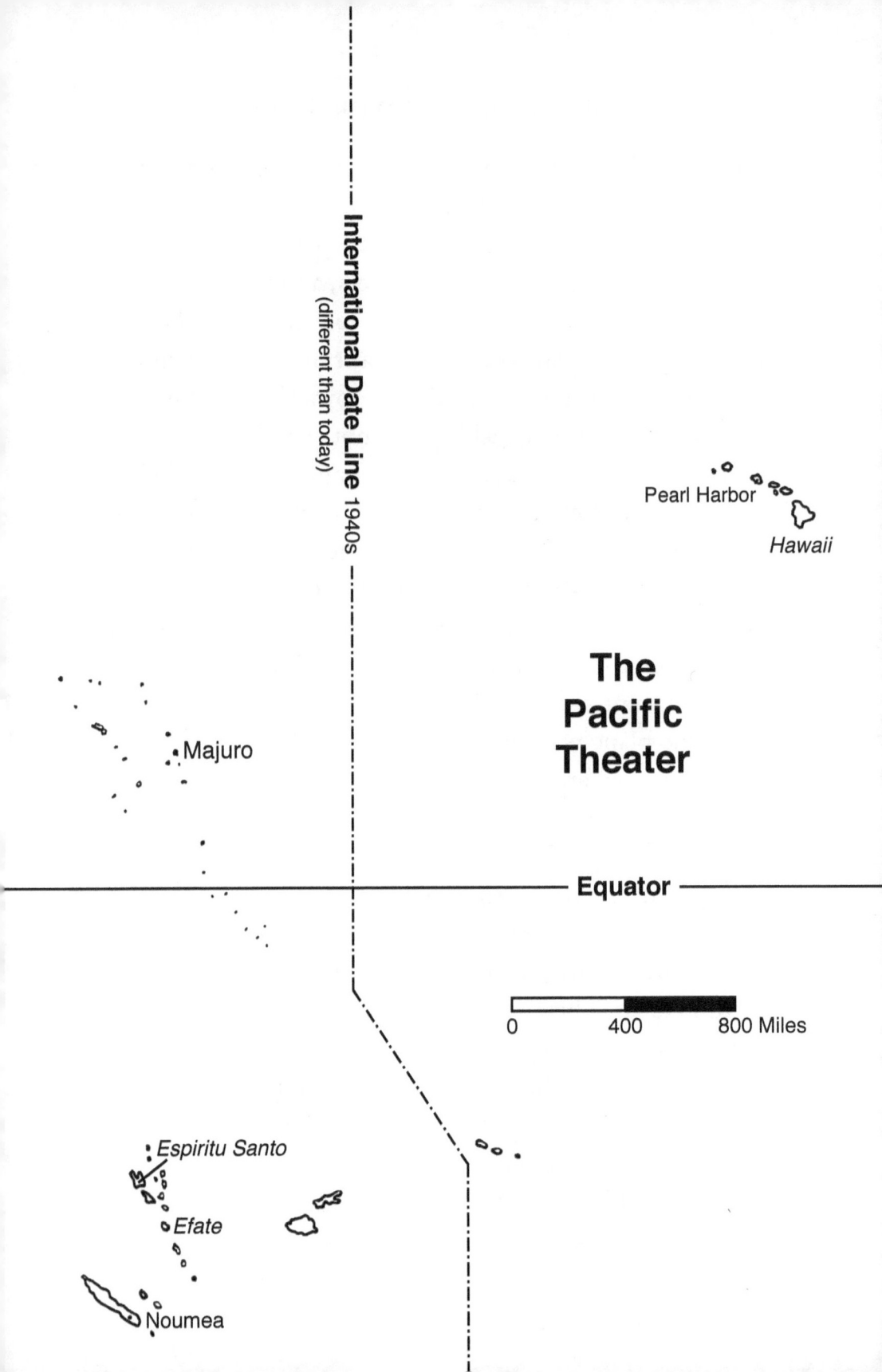

these were held frequently now—and she stepped to the porthole of her cabin to look out.

From here she could see a good part of the United States battle fleet: cruisers, destroyers, and the great, gray battleships tied up close together alongside Ford Island. On the deck of the *Nevada* several sailors were fishing. Overhead an airplane was diving toward them but the sailors, intent on their fishing, did not even look up.

Later it would seem to Lieutenant Lally that what followed was something she had dreamed or seen in a movie. Along the leading edge of the plane's wing little blinking lights began to flash. Instinctively Grace Lally knew they were guns. At the same time one of the sailors fishing on the *Nevada* shuddered and fell backward. Another went stumbling across the deck before he fell. Then the plane was gone and Grace Lally stared after it, uncertain of what she had seen. Had that really been a red circle painted on the wing—the emblem of Japan?

Grace Lally turned and ran from her cabin to the wardroom. The windows were wide here, the view better. Before one of the windows the ship's paymaster stood as if frozen. Miss Lally joined him. Neither spoke. There was no time for it. They watched an airplane come out of the sky in a long, steeply slanting dive. They saw the bomb detach itself from the plane's belly and flash downward to strike the battleship *Arizona*. A great mass of flame and smoke blotted out the sky.

There could no longer be any doubt in Grace Lally's mind. I must get the emergency wards set up, she thought. Her voice was quite calm and steady as she began giving orders to the young nurses who came running into the wardroom. Soon the officers' lounge, where members of the crew had been gathering for the church service a few minutes before, was filled with sixty-seven double-decker bunks. Other beds were set up in the crew's recreation room, even on the open decks. Blood plasma bottles, drugs, bandages were piled ready.

Around the *Solace* bombs were still falling. Ships burned and exploded. Guns roared at the flashing planes. But Grace Lally and her twelve nurses had no time to look or listen. Already the wounded were being brought aboard.

☩

The hospital in the navy yard at Pearl Harbor was an old but pretty building on a hill above the harbor. The Sick Officers' Quarters were on the second deck, and shortly before eight o'clock Ensign Ann Davidson stood at one of the windows looking out. It was a beautiful morning, she thought. Hibiscus and frangipani bloomed in the yard below her. Yellow-billed myna birds hopped about on the grass. Above the harbor the sky was an incredible blue.

Ann Davidson sighed and turned away from the window. In her starched white uniform she was a very efficient nurse and it was time now for work.

From behind her, somewhere out over the harbor, came the sound of guns. Like Grace Lally, dressing for church on the *Solace*, Ann paid little attention at first. Just another air raid drill, she thought.

Abruptly the whole building quivered. From the harbor came the sound of explosions, one after another. Ann ran to the lanai, the wide porch that extended the full length of the quarters. Other nurses were here, and medical corpsmen, even some patients wearing their hospital pajamas. All were leaning over the rail, stretching their necks to look upward.

They heard the planes before they saw them, a heavy, rumbling thunder that made the building shake. Then the planes swept into view: dark brown, so low they barely cleared the roof of the hospital, the red emblem of Japan clearly visible on the wings as they flashed downward toward the harbor and the long line of anchored battleships. Moments later the ships were wrapped in billowing clouds of flame and smoke as the torpedoes struck.

All the guns in the harbor were firing now. Shrapnel began to rain on the roof of the hospital and in the yard. Someone on the lanai cried, "Look!" and Ann Davidson saw, high overhead, a plane spiraling downward with a banner of smoke streaming behind it. Fire mingled with the smoke. The spiraling plane seemed to grow suddenly large in Ann's eyes. It hurtled straight toward the hospital, missed, crashed through a hedge of scarlet hibiscus flowers, and burst into fragments that showered on the tennis court and on a row of rabbit pens beyond.

Somewhere a man said, his voice sounding strangely calm, "We are at war."

Ann's first impulse was to run, to hide from the sound of the guns, the bombs, the great rumbling explosions that went on and on in the harbor. Then she forced herself to be still. She forced her hands to stop trembling. I have a job to do, she thought. We've had drills to prepare us for this. I know what my work is.

She turned quietly back into the Sick Officers' Quarters. A lieutenant was sitting on a bed, hacking with a pocketknife at the plaster cast on his knee. Before Ann could speak he had knocked the cast free. "I've got to get back to my ship," he said, and was gone. The next bed was also empty. It had held a navy doctor whose appendix had been removed three days before. Later Ann would learn that he had gone straight to the operating room and had worked two days without relief.

There were other patients, however, who had to be taken care of. Those who could walk were moved to tents set up by corpsmen on the lawn. Bed patients were carried on stretchers to the basement, making room for the casualties soon to arrive.

By nine o'clock these casualties began to reach the hospital. Some came in ambulances, one load after another. Some were brought on stretchers directly from the harbor's edge. Soon they filled the beds. They filled row after row of mattresses laid on the floor.

Ann Davidson worked as she had never worked before. She and the other nurses cut away uniforms soaked with blood and oil. They gave morphine to ease the pain of the wounded. They cleaned shell wounds and horrible burns. They gave blood transfusions. As soon as one person was taken to an operating room, the nurses tore the bloody sheets off the bed, replaced them with clean linen, and motioned for corpsmen to bring another patient. In the operating rooms doctors and nurses worked steadily, not even pausing between patients.

Ann lost track of time. She was surprised when a corpsman handed her a bowl of soup. "Here," he said. "You'll need this before the job is over." She drank the soup and went back to work.

Night came but there was no letup in the work. New casualties were still being brought from the burned and battered ships. The windows of the operating rooms had been hastily painted black so that no light would show outside. In the wards the nurses moved swiftly among the crowded beds and blood-stained mattresses, carrying flashlights covered with blue paper. No one knew when or if a second attack might come. Wild rumors swept the hospital: Japanese troops were landing on the north side of the island; they were landing on the south side of the island; they were being dropped by parachute. Guns in the harbor were quiet, then suddenly began to fire, then fell quiet again.

✣

On board the *Solace* there was a sudden alarm when American antisubmarine craft began to swarm around the hospital ship. Depth charges hurled great geysers of water into the air. The *Solace* rocked with the explosions. A pale-faced nurse told Grace Lally, "I heard one of the officers say there is a Japanese submarine hiding right underneath us. We may be sunk by our own ships trying to get the submarine."

"Nonsense," replied the Chief Nurse. "And we don't have time for nonsense now. Help get these patients ready for the operating room."

So the work went on. At the old hospital in the navy yard Ann Davidson felt someone touch her arm. It was her friend Catherine Richardson. "Lie down over there in the corner and sleep an hour," Catherine said. "Then I'll wake you and you can let me sleep an hour."

"All right."

It was the only rest either would get that night. The next day, Monday, was almost as bad. It was Tuesday before the number of patients waiting for the operating rooms began to thin out—before the nurses, staggering with exhaustion, could sleep more than an hour or two at a time.

By then the war had already moved on. There would be no second attack on Hawaii. But in the Philippines the army and navy nurses were already facing an even more dangerous and terrible situation than those in Pearl Harbor had faced.

The International Date Line lies between Hawaii and the Philippines. When it was eight A.M. on December 7 in Hawaii, it was three A.M., December 8, in the Philippines.

On Corregidor Island, the army's fortress guarding Manila Bay, Second Lieutenant Ruth Stoltz, a nurse from Dayton, Ohio, slept peacefully. It was daylight when she awoke and her friend Minnie Breese, who had joined the service with her, was standing beside her bed.

"Wake up!" Minnie said. She had been on night duty and had only now come from the hospital. "The Japanese have bombed Pearl Harbor!"

Ruth yawned. "I don't care if—" She stopped. "What did you say?"

"The Japanese have bombed Pearl Harbor. We're at war!"

"I don't believe it," Ruth said. She had known, of course, that the United States and Japan might go to war. But she had believed, as did everyone else—and this included the admirals and generals—that if war did come, it would begin with a Japanese attack on the Philippines, not Pearl Harbor. "I don't believe it," she said again.

"Get up to the hospital. You'll find out."

Corregidor is a small, tadpole-shaped island, so hilly that the nurses and soldiers living there divided it into three sections called Topside, Middleside, and Bottomside. The hospital was on Middleside. There were only a few patients and little work to do. The morning slipped by in a kind of eerie calm. The only planes that passed overhead were American planes going out to search for the enemy. They found nothing and returned to their airfields about noon.

✚

Shortly after noon Second Lieutenant Dorothea Daley was reading a newspaper in the office of the Fort Stotsenberg Hospital, across Manila Bay from Corregidor. She had been in the Philippines only a few months, but that had been long enough for her to meet and fall in love with Lieutenant Emanuel "Boots" Engel. Boots was stationed at Clark Field, only a half mile from Fort Stotsenberg Hospital. As Dorothea read about the bombing of Pearl Harbor she wondered what this war would mean to her and Boots.

Suddenly the building shook so that a mirror fell off the wall. Medicine bottles spilled from a shelf. Dorothea jumped to her feet. There had been no siren, no warning of any kind. But now she could hear the explosions: a long, steady, rumbling thunder of sound. From the hospital porch someone shouted, "The Japanese are bombing Clark Field!"

"Boots!" Dorothea thought. He was at Clark Field. She started to pray, silently, even while she ran toward the ward where she would be needed.

Within half an hour the casualties began to arrive. They came in ambulance after ambulance. They came in automobiles and trucks. They came limping, stumbling across the hospital lawn. For the nurses at Fort Stotsenberg it was much as it had been at Pearl Harbor: there was the burned and bloody clothing to be cut away, morphine and blood transfusions to be given, beds made and unmade. There were the rows of silent men waiting to be carried into the operating rooms where the work went on and on.

For Dorothea there was an added terror. Each time she turned to a new patient she wondered, Is it Boots? Will he be blind, maimed? What will I say to him?

The work went on, all through the afternoon and night, but Boots was not among the wounded. Dorothea had no way of knowing what had happened to him or where he was.

On Corregidor, Ruth Stoltz and the other nurses learned of the Japanese attack on the Philippine airfields. They heard that almost all of the American planes had been caught on the ground and destroyed. But on Corregidor the afternoon passed in the same strange calm as the morning. Night came. The sky was clear with bright moonlight. Nurses going from their quarters up the tiered steps to the hospital wore white uniforms, and the uniforms gleamed in the moonlight. A colonel saw them. "You want to be killed?" he shouted. "A Japanese pilot could see you a mile away! Change those uniforms!"

To Ruth Stoltz, looking down the flower-covered slopes of the island to the calm, moonlit bay, it seemed impossible that anyone should try to kill them. She would learn better in the days that followed.

BATAAN AND CORREGIDOR
CHAPTER TWO

After most of the American aircraft in the Philippines had been destroyed on the ground, Japanese troops began to pour into the islands. Without air cover the American and Filipino soldiers were pushed back. Soon the Japanese had captured all of Luzon, the main Philippine island, except Bataan. This is a narrow, mountainous, jungle-covered peninsula along the western side of Manila Bay, its southern tip only a few miles across the water from Corregidor. All the army and navy nurses who had been on Luzon were sent to Bataan or to Corregidor.

On Bataan the nurses did not find any beautiful, well-equipped hospitals waiting for them. At a place called Limay near the coast there were some old barracks buildings. With soap and water, scrub brushes, and elbow grease these were converted into a hospital. A second hospital, called simply Number Two, was set up deep in the jungle with even fewer facilities.

Dorothea Daley was stationed at Limay. She had not seen Boots since the bombing of Clark Field. Once she had heard that he was still alive, uninjured. But with the fighting growing steadily worse there was no way to be sure from minute to minute.

The hospital at Limay had 500 beds, cots placed so close together there was scarcely room for the nurses to move between them. Soon there were 1600 patients, with more pouring in each day. The cots were converted into double-deckers, then triple-deckers. The nurses had to climb on stools or ladders to reach the patients in the top bunks. Always Dorothea searched each new face, both hopeful and afraid. Sometimes there would be a casualty with his face half shot away, or so badly burned as to be unrecognizable. With shaking hands she would look at the tag that had been tied to his clothing at the first-aid station near the lines. But days and weeks passed and she did not see or hear of Boots.

One of the main roads on Bataan passed near the hospital. Japanese planes flew up and down it, bombing anything that moved. Sometimes the bombs fell so near the hospital that the buildings shook. Antiaircraft guns, firing at the planes, sprayed shrapnel over the area. When the bombs and shrapnel were falling, the nurses who were off duty dived into foxholes. But for those on duty there was not even the protection of a foxhole. They stayed with

their patients. Sometimes the nurses stretched out on the floor between the cots until the bombing was over, then went back to work. In the operating rooms, where the work could not stop even for a while, the doctors and nurses learned to ignore the fear that ate at them—and to keep going.

The white uniforms of the nurses had long since given way to steel helmets, khaki trousers, khaki shirts, and GI shoes. Of these the army had just three sizes, the nurses said: too small, too big, and—most plentiful of all—too too big. Even so, the nurses tried to keep themselves as optimistic as possible. And indeed they were appreciated by the wounded, half-starved soldiers brought back from the front lines. To these wounded, the mere fact that an American nurse was here, taking care of them, was a great boost to morale.

Food was a serious problem on Bataan from the first. In the hospitals the nurses were served only two meals a day. Soon they all began to lose weight. Dorothea Daley was worried that if ever she did see Boots again she would look, as she said, "like a skinned chicken."

But if there was a shortage of food for the nurses, it was even worse for the soldiers on the front lines. Food was the first thing the casualties would ask for when they reached the hospitals. This was usually at night because the Japanese bombed everything on the roads in the daytime, including ambulances.

"Nurse, can I have something to eat? I haven't eaten in two days."

"Can't you wait until breakfast? It's not long."

"I'm awfully hungry. The last thing I had to eat was a bowl of rice and some roots I dug up in the jungle."

Then the nurse might go to look for Lieutenant Juanita Redmond, a small woman who was in charge of the kitchen when she was not working in the operating rooms. "Red, these new casualties are starving. Can't you find something for them?"

And Juanita Redmond would find something, though the supplies got lower and lower each day.

There came a brief lull in the fighting, and with it life at the two hospitals grew less hectic for a while. With a few hours off each day, doctors and nurses would go to the beach for a swim. They would take picnic lunches. These might be nothing but a can of fruit or a few wild bananas. Or it might be a chicken that one of the doctors had bought from a Filipino native and they would cook it over an open fire.

Once Juanita Redmond and Lieutenant Inez MacDonald had a chance to visit the navy gunboat *Canopus* where it was hidden under camouflage close against the bay shore. After Bataan it seemed strange to sit at a table with clean linen and polished silver, to laugh and talk with the young officers and dance to phonograph music. It seemed very peaceful—and yet all of them knew that Japanese planes and submarines were searching for the *Canopus* at that very moment. They knew that any minute a torpedo or bomb might strike. But it did no good to think about these things. Like most of the nurses, they had adopted the philosophy of Old Pop, the army cook at the Limay Hospital. "If a bomb's gonna get ya," Pop said, "it's gonna get ya. If it's not, it's not. So there's no need to worry about it."

It was during this brief lull in the fighting that Dorothea Daley looked up from her work one day and saw Boots standing in front of her. For a moment she could only stare at him. Then with a cry she threw her arms around him. "What are you doing here? Are you wounded? Where did you come from? Where have you been?"

He began to laugh. "I'm not wounded. But one of our men was, and I learned from him that you were here. I got a day's leave and hitchhiked a ride to see you."

Boots was stationed at Mariveles at the southern tip of Bataan. This was not far away, and whenever possible he would get a ride on a passing truck and visit Dorothea. Because their time together was so rare, it seemed even more wonderful than before.

The lull in the fighting ended. Once more the Japanese troops were driving forward, pushing the Americans and Filipinos back. Soon the front lines were so close that all day long the nurses could hear the guns booming. Shells began to fall closer and closer. Finally came word that the hospital would have to move. Patients had to be put in casts so they could stand the jolting over rough roads. They had to be loaded into ambulances, trucks, anything that would carry them. Traveling at night, they moved southward down the peninsula.

The new hospital was called Little Baguio. It was in the mountains and the weather here was cooler than it had been at Limay. But the hospital itself was even more crude.

Some of the buildings had once served as garages for army trucks. Some were merely sheds, with neither walls nor floors. Strong winds blew dust over everything—over the beds, over the wounded, over the food as they tried to eat. By now the food situation had become critical. For a while there had been carabao (water buffalo) meat. It was tough and strong-tasting, but it was meat. Then it gave out and for several days there was no meat at all.

One of the mess attendants at the hospital had formerly been a member of the 27th Philippine Scout Cavalry. This unit had been so badly shot to pieces that it had to be broken up. For a while the horses and mules were used to carry supplies. Then one day the nurses at Little Baguio were served meat that tasted like nothing they had eaten before. One of them asked the mess-sergeant, "Is this beef?"

"No, Lieutenant."

"What is it?"

The sergeant shook his head sadly. "Twenty-seventh Cavalry, Lieutenant."

All the nurses stopped eating. "You mean horse meat?" one of them asked.

The sergeant nodded.

The nurses pushed back their plates. They looked at one another, then at the meat. "If we don't eat it," one of them said, "it means we don't eat anything at all." And they started eating again.

The men in the lines did not even have horse meat. Sometimes they killed a wild monkey in the jungle and ate it. Sometimes they killed a snake or a wild pig. But often the only food was a handful of rice, and sometimes not that. Weakened by hunger, the men came down with diseases such as scurvy and beriberi. Often the only water available was in muddy creeks or ponds. Amebic dysentery and diarrhea spread rapidly. Worst of all, however, was malaria. Within three months after the fighting started on Bataan, a thousand malaria patients were pouring into the hospitals every day. And the quinine needed for treatment was rapidly giving out.

Among the soldiers, among the doctors and nurses, all the talk now was about help from the United States. Surely, they said, help must be on the way. But when would it arrive? Could it get here in time? Wild rumors swept the two hospitals: a fleet of battleships and airplane carriers had been seen approaching from the east; they had been seen coming from Australia in the south; ships were coming from China in the west.

The truth was that most American battleships had been destroyed or put out of commission in the attack on Pearl Harbor. At this time the United States simply did not have a fleet that could challenge the Japanese. In Washington, President Roosevelt and his advisers had slowly, painfully, made their decision: no help could be sent to the Philippines.

Gradually the men and women on Bataan and Corregidor came to realize this. There would be no help. They must hold out as long as possible. After that...

No one wanted to think about what would happen after that.

About this time a baby was born in the Little Baguio Hospital on Bataan. The mother was the Filipino wife of a soldier nearby. Any baby born under such circumstances needed a very special name, the nurses thought. The mother was willing to accept any name the nurses chose, and for days they talked and argued about it. Finally the baby was named Victoria Bataana. She was the darling of the entire hospital. Not only the nurses but even the doctors and wounded soldiers wanted to carry her, feed her, look after her. When finally the mother took her home, everyone tried to find some small gift to send with her.

And it was at this time that Dorothea Daley and Boots Engel decided to be married. Perhaps they might live through the days that lay ahead, perhaps not. The future was too uncertain to waste the present. Later Dorothea would write:

On February 19, 1942, I, Dorothea Mae Daley, took Emanuel Engel, Jr., to be my wedded husband, for better, for worse, in sickness or in health, till death do us part. Everybody in the wedding party, including the bride, was in khaki. I had covered my khaki pants with a khaki skirt which one of the nurses had concocted and which she loaned to me for my wedding night.... Sounds of bombs were in the distance, and my feet, encased in huge army boots, felt awkward as I stood in an army hospital the like of which had never been seen before.... But there was a solemnity and a sacredness about the ceremony, performed in the midst of such tragedy, that made us both feel that ours was no ordinary marriage. We had taken vows which can never be broken.

There was a six-hour honeymoon. Then Boots went back to Mariveles and Dorothea back to her work in the hospital. That work was harder than ever now. The hospital overflowed with sick and wounded. Even the open sheds would no longer hold them. Some were in tents. Some lay on cots and mattresses under the trees. The "hospital" was strung out for three miles through the jungle.

Every day the Japanese army pushed closer. Always now there was the sound of guns, the roar of enemy airplanes passing overhead. The hospital at Little Baguio was marked by huge red crosses painted on sheets and on the roofs of the sheds, clearly visible to the planes overhead. Under international law these crosses meant that the place was unarmed, and in turn should not be attacked. So far the Japanese had respected this agreement.

Early one morning Ensign Ann Bernatitus, a navy nurse, was crossing the hospital compound toward the operating rooms when she heard the growing rumble of planes. They were close and getting closer. Ann looked up, and saw a plane hurtling out of the morning sky as if it were aimed straight for her. There was no time to think. Instinctively she dived head first into a foxhole. An instant later the first bomb fell, then another. And another. The ground, the air, the whole earth was a shuddering, rumbling, roaring thunder.

It passed. Ann looked up. The hospital wards, directly

in front of her, had not been hit but other buildings were on fire. Somewhere toward the main road men were screaming. Ann jumped up and began to run toward the operating rooms. A soldier shouted at her, "Get down! Here come more planes!" But she kept running, knowing that she would be needed in the operating rooms. The bombs crashed somewhere behind her.

Ann was working alongside Lieutenant Commander Smith and Lieutenant Fraleigh, navy surgeons, when a second wave of planes came over. As the buildings shook with the explosions, the patient on the operating table—who had received a local anesthetic—moved his head slowly to one side. "Doc," he said, "get under the table. There's no need of you people being killed because of me.

"If they kill me," Commander Smith said, "it will be while I'm working." He looked at Ann. "Bernatitus, you'd better find a foxhole until this is over."

Ann's smile was a bit shaky at the edges, but it was a smile. "I'm not as big a target as you are," she said, and kept working.

That night the Japanese apologized by radio for bombing the hospital. It had, the Japanese said, been a mistake. Everyone at Little Baguio hoped so. They put out more and bigger red crosses.

On Easter Monday, Juanita Redmond was working in one of the wards when someone shouted, "Planes overhead!" In the same instant a bomb fell so close that the concussion knocked her down. She staggered up, slightly groggy. The building had not been hit, but corpsmen were running out, carrying stretchers. More bombs were falling, though not as close as the first one. Casualties began to arrive.

Outside the ward someone shouted, "They're coming back!"

Swiftly Juanita began to help wounded men get out of their cots to lie on the floor. In the orthopedic ward other nurses were cutting traction ropes so the patients could roll out of their beds onto the floor. Then came the thin, terrible whine of a bomb close overhead. A sergeant grabbed Juanita Redmond and pulled her under a desk. As she hit the floor, the floor seemed to rise up and hurl her into the air. She had a weird feeling of turning over and over in space.

She was on the floor again—or on what had been a floor. She could hear the sound of her own breathing. Her eyes felt too big for their sockets. Somewhere a man was calling, "Where's Miss Redmond? Is Miss Redmond all right?" She recognized the voice. It was that of a soldier who had lost both legs and whom she had been nursing.

"I'm all right," she said, though she wasn't sure. She got to her feet. The roof of the ward was blown away, the floor ripped into fragments. Men lay sprawled about, some newly wounded, some dead. Rosemary Hogan, one of Juanita's closest friends, passed her, led by a soldier. Blood streamed from Rosemary's face and from one shoulder. "Hogan," Juanita asked, "is it bad?"

Rosemary waved her good arm. "Just a nosebleed. I hope."

The bombers were gone. They left behind an almost demolished hospital. Nine out of every ten beds had been smashed. Most of the buildings had been destroyed. Three nurses were wounded so badly that they had to be sent to Corregidor.

And yet those who remained continued to work. Not only were there the casualties from the bombing, but new ones from the front were constantly arriving. And the front was very close now. All night the nurses could hear the sound of rifle fire. Everyone knew the Japanese might break through and capture the hospital at any time. Four months had passed since the bombing of Pearl Harbor.

Early on the night of April 8 the nurses were called from their duties. Chief Nurse Josephine Nesbitt told them they were being sent to Mariveles. From there they would get a boat to Corregidor. They must be ready to leave in an hour, taking only what they could carry themselves. (Doctors and corpsmen would stay behind with the patients.)

No one would forget the night that followed. The nurses rode on trucks, jeeps, cars, anything they could get aboard. If the truck or car broke down, they walked. The roads were clogged with soldiers, some going in one direction, some another. There were wounded men, limping, heads or arms or legs in bandages. Some were blind, being led by friends. And as the night passed, the sky over Bataan turned into a gigantic, flame-colored fireworks display. The American army was destroying its own supplies to keep them from being captured by the Japanese. Gasoline and ammunition dumps exploded. Shells hurtled high in the sky and burst like Roman candles.

It was well after daylight when most of the nurses reached Mariveles. And here they were told the last boat for Corregidor had gone! Because of the Japanese planes nothing could cross the open water in daylight.

What now? The nurses looked at one another wondering. Yet most of them were too completely exhausted to worry. And Japanese planes were coming over. The nurses took refuge in ditches alongside the road. Within minutes most of them were asleep.

Dorothea Daley (it still seemed strange to her that she was Mrs. Engel now) kept hoping she would see Boots. He was supposed to be at Mariveles. But there was no sign of him, and after a while she too went to sleep alongside the road.

She was awakened by somebody cheering. A boat had come. It wasn't much of a boat, but perhaps it would get them to Corregidor. The nurses piled aboard, the boat pushed off from the dock—and moments later a Japanese airplane came slicing down out of the sky.

One bomb missed the boat. Another hit the dock where the nurses had been minutes before. The dock exploded into bits. The plane went on, disappearing over the mountains while the small boat ran for Corregidor two miles away.

Life on the small island in the bay was not much safer than it had been on Bataan. Japanese planes flew overhead at will. Japanese artillery, now based on Bataan, shelled the island day and night. The hospital at Middleside had long since been wrecked and abandoned. A new hospital was set up in some of the tunnels that honeycombed the island hills.

One night a seaplane slipped in through the darkness, bringing a few supplies. When it flew away, heading for Australia, it took a few of the nurses with it. A submarine picked up a few others. Those who were rescued included Ensign Ann Bernatitus, Lieutenant Juanita Redmond, and Lieutenant Dorothea Daley Engel. Since leaving Bataan, Dorothea had no word of Boots. (She would never see him again. Later she would learn he had died while a Japanese prisoner.)

Most of the nurses remained on Corregidor, carrying on their work as best they could. They were always hungry. Food, medicine, even ammunition were rapidly giving out. Everyone knew the Japanese would soon invade the island. There was talk of fighting to the last man, from tunnel to tunnel. If so, what would happen to the nurses?

There was no answer.

Ruth Stoltz was one of the few nurses who had been

on Corregidor since the first day of the war. Quietly now she went about her work. And there was a great deal of work. The hospital tunnels were jammed with casualties, with new ones arriving almost constantly. There was no air conditioning. Fans brought in only a little fresh air. Always there was heat, and the odor of disinfectants, of draining wounds, of ether and unwashed bodies. Dust covered everything, no matter how hard the nurses and corpsmen worked.

Sometimes, in the few spare moments available, Ruth would go outside the tunnel to breathe the fresh air. But outside the tunnel there was always danger. The shelling, she thought, was worse than the bombing because there was no warning: just a thin, wailing whine and instants later the crash of the shell. Sometimes the shelling went on for hours, and stopped, and began again without warning. It was, Ruth thought, like living on a bull's-eye.

Little by little the island's defenses were destroyed.

On the night of May 5, 1942, Japanese troops landed on Corregidor. Against the poorly armed, half-starved Americans they pushed rapidly forward. By noon next day General Jonathan Wainwright, the American commander, had made his decision. It was no longer possible to defend the island. To save the remainder of his forces from being slaughtered, he surrendered.

Working deep in the tunnels the nurses could not know just what was happening. From the new casualties pouring into the underground hospital they learned that the

Japanese had landed; they knew the Americans were being pushed back. They knew also that their duty was to look after the casualties, and they kept working.

Ruth Stoltz was bending over a newly wounded man when she became aware of the silence. It was as sudden as a shell burst. She looked up and saw a Japanese officer walking down the tunnel. After him came Japanese soldiers, carrying rifles with bayonets. Swaggering, they came down the narrow aisle between the cots of the wounded men. Without a word they passed Ruth and went out of the other end of the tunnel. The nurse turned back to her work. She knew now that she was a Japanese prisoner. How long that prison life would last, or what it would be like, she could not foresee.

ENGLAND
CHAPTER THREE

Even before the United States went to war, both the army and navy were short of nurses. Men were being drafted into the armed services, but not women. To meet the shortage, the government appealed to young registered nurses to volunteer for duty. Each R.N. who did so would be given the rank of a commissioned officer, second lieutenant in the army or ensign in the navy.

One of those who joined almost a year before the war began was Theresa Archard. She was sent to Camp Shelby, in Mississippi. At this time the camp was still being built. Jeeps and trucks churned up and down streets that alternated between deep mud and deeper dust. Along the streets, raw frame buildings sprang up like mushrooms. The nurses' quarters were in a barracks building as sparsely furnished as a barn. The hospital was still unfinished; there were beds in the wards with patients in them, but carpenters were passing back and forth between the beds. The air was filled with the banging of hammers and the smell of fresh paint.

Despite the confusion, the nurses' work was much as it would have been in any civilian hospital, except that the patients were practically all young, and all men. And in an amazingly short time the hospital building was finished. Soon there was new furniture in the nurses' quarters. Things took on a homey look. Indeed, by early December everything seemed so peaceful that Theresa Archard, half bored, was looking forward to the end of her enlistment. She had a new car and was eager to travel. Her best friend, Dorothy Pridham, however, had decided to re-enlist.

On the night of December 6, they talked it over. "The government only asked that we join for one year," Theresa said. "If every nurse would give one year of voluntary service, the boys would be taken care of."

"But not enough nurses are joining," Prid said. "What if we had a war?"

"I don't think there will be one."

Next afternoon Theresa knew differently. Over the radio the news was repeated time and again: the Japanese had bombed Pearl Harbor. "Well," Theresa told her friend, "that settles it. I can't quit now."

Four days later a notice was posted outside the Chief Nurse's office: NURSES WISHING TO VOLUNTEER FOR OVERSEAS DUTY SIGN BELOW. Theresa and Dorothy

Pridham read it together. They looked at each other. "All right," Theresa said. "We are in it. We might as well go where the real work is."

They both signed their names.

No nurse who sailed for England that spring or summer of 1942 would ever forget the experience. However, it is doubtful if any one of them could ever remember all the details. Things were too confused. There was too much rush, stop, and rush again. For many of the women this was their first introduction to the ancient military rule, "Hurry up and wait."

First there was the train ride from the army camp or navy base to the Port of Embarkation, usually New York. Then there was the problem of finding the proper army or navy office. And then there was what appeared to be total chaos: hundreds, thousands of people who had never seen one another before, all going in different directions and apparently all lost.

Yet, somehow, things got done. One bunch of nurses would find themselves in line getting inoculations: tetanus, typhoid, typhus, all at once, two in one arm and one in the other. Other nurses would be signing up for equipment: a sack-like object called a musette bag for carrying personal articles, a gas mask, a steel helmet, a mess kit, a canteen belt, a bedroll.

The bedroll was a huge canvas mat with leather straps and with pockets at each end. "In the field," the nurses were told, "this may have to serve as both bed and trunk. So watch closely and learn how to pack it."

One group of nurses, from a camp in Tennessee, found that their foot lockers containing their summer uniforms had not arrived in time. They were issued new winter uniforms, then had to wear them in the broiling heat of New York summer.

Finally sailing orders would come through. The nurses, wearing their winter uniforms, with gas masks, helmets, musette bags, and canteen belts hung about them, carrying overcoats and suitcases, would stagger out of the hotels where they had been quartered. They would pile into buses for the ride to the docks. There they would stagger off the buses and across the docks, across railroad tracks, across more docks, until finally the great ships loomed ahead of them and they went panting up the gangplanks.

For most of the nurses the voyage across the Atlantic was a sort of combination nightmare and fancy-dress ball. The ships were crowded with soldiers; usually there was dancing on deck in the afternoons and in the officers' lounge at night. Couples strolled the decks in the moonlight, and there was the start of many a romance. Yet at the same time everyone knew that German submarines lay in wait for the convoys. They knew that disaster or even death might strike at any moment. Each nurse had to wear her canteen belt with the canteen full of water at all times: if the ship were sunk, that canteen might mean the difference between life and death to someone drifting in a small boat. Life jackets had to be worn or carried everywhere, even to meals. The jackets were put carefully beside the bunks at night, ready to be grabbed at a moment's notice.

Day and night there were abandon-ship drills—and nobody knew when the next one might be real.

Most of the nurses made the journey safely and happily. But for one group, called the Harvard Unit, the nightmare suddenly became real. Their ship was passing through waters so cold that now and then icebergs could be seen drifting past. Submarines haunted its course. Suddenly, the big ship shuddered. There was a tremendous roar as a torpedo tore into it. Flames spread quickly. Through the smoke and darkness the nurses groped their way to their lifeboat stations.

Mary Ann Sullivan, a slender, brown-haired nurse from Boston, fought down the fear that gripped her. I won't panic, she told herself; I won't panic! She looked at the other nurses lined up on either side. Fear showed in their faces; yet quietly, steadily, they obeyed orders as if this were simply another drill.

Along with sailors, soldiers, and other nurses, Mary Ann climbed into the lifeboat assigned to her. Huge, icy waves threatened to smash it against the side of the sinking ship. Then the small boat was clear, rising and falling with the swells.

Later the occupants of the lifeboat were picked up by another ship. Somewhat frostbitten but otherwise uninjured, Mary Ann was carried to Iceland. From there she and the other nurses continued their journey to England.

England was a strange, new world for most of the American nurses. The country had been at war for almost three years. Food, clothing, even cosmetics were rationed. Lieutenant Ruth Haskell, walking along a city street, noticed that all the women turned to look after her. They seemed to be staring at her legs. "What's wrong with me?" she thought. "Am I suddenly bowlegged or something?"

Finally an English girl explained to her. "It's your silk stockings, Miss. In England we haven't seen silk stockings in so long we can't help but stare at them. They are so pretty."

Other things made the war seem even closer and more ominous. The 2nd General Hospital, where Marjorie Peto

of New Jersey was the Chief Nurse, was located near a large airfield. Night after night airplanes roared overhead and the girls learned to tell the sound of their own planes from those of the Germans. They learned to recognize the sound of an American or English plane when it was in trouble returning from a raid. Many of the nurses had made friends among the pilots. They could imagine the men in the crippled plane limping through the night sky. In the blacked-out hospital below, the nurses would listen intently, saying silent prayers for the fliers.

When the planes overhead were German and the air raid sirens howled in the night, all the nurses, on and off duty, had to go to their stations. Chief Nurse Peto insisted they wear their helmets. "We have a lot more casualties from bumping into things in the blackout," she said, "than we do from German bombs."

Not all the American nurses sent to England were assigned to hospitals at first. Many of them, like Ruth Haskell and Theresa Archard who were with the 48th Surgical, were sent to live in long rows of prefabricated

buildings. Here the girls would be turned out of bed early in the morning to take exercise. Then there was breakfast, then classes, drill, lunch, and still more drill. This went on day after day, and the afternoon marches got longer and longer. Sometimes the nurses had to carry heavy packs while they marched. Frequently they staggered back to their Nissen huts with feet badly blistered and sometimes bleeding.

Since there was no actual nursing to be done, many of the girls thought they were wasting their time. "I joined the nurse corps, not the infantry," one of them told Ruth Haskell. "I don't see why I have to walk ten miles in an afternoon, and loaded like a burro."

Lieutenant Haskell smiled, a little ruefully. "The colonel says this will come in handy later on. But I hope not."

Life, however, was not all marching. Nearby army posts, both British and American, often gave dances. A blanket invitation would be sent to all the nurses at a hospital or camp. The nurses would get all dressed up— and then climb into the back of a big truck to be driven through the blacked-out countryside to the army post. After the dance they would climb back into the truck to return to their own camp.

Now and then each girl would be given a few days' leave to go sightseeing. She might visit Coventry or London, and stare in awe at the horrible wreckage caused by German bombs. She might visit places she had read and heard about all her life: Shakespeare's birthplace at Stratford-on-Avon, or Westminster Abbey, where so many of England's famous men and women are buried, or Stonehenge with its tremendous, mysterious stones. And Marjorie Peto, as Chief Nurse of 2nd General, even received an invitation to Buckingham Palace, along with other American officers. There she met the king and queen and young Princess Margaret Rose.

Even so, many of the nurses not assigned to active hospitals were becoming impatient. "I came over here to nurse," Ruth Haskell told a friend. "Instead, all we do is drill. There are just too many nurses in England."

She did not know that, even as she talked, the American and British High Commands were planning to invade North Africa. Very soon Lieutenant Haskell, along with the other nurses and doctors and corpsmen of the 48th Surgical, would find herself right in the middle of some of the most terrible action of the entire war.

NORTH AFRICA
CHAPTER FOUR

The order came suddenly. The 48th Surgical was moving. Just where they were going was top secret; but everybody in the unit felt sure it would be close to the fighting. For one thing, the nurses could not take their foot lockers with them. They would take bedrolls, gas masks, canteens, musette bags, whatever they could carry. And that was all.

The move began with a night march of two and a half miles, the girls stumbling through the darkness, loaded down with their packs. Then there was an eighteen-hour train ride. The nurses slept in their seats or on the floor. From the train they trudged wearily to a ship already jammed with soldiers. The ship put to sea, joining a convoy so huge it stretched from horizon to horizon.

And still none of them knew where they were going.

Life on the ship was pleasant enough. The food was good. The double-decker bunks, though crowded, were clean. The officers were attentive, and once more there were the beginnings of romances.

There were frequent life-boat drills. Theresa Archard, now promoted to Chief Nurse of the 48th Surgical's second unit, always checked to make sure her nurses wore their life jackets. In fact, on one occasion she was so busy checking the others that she forgot to wear her own. It was an embarrassing moment.

Two weeks passed. Then word spread swiftly through the ship: they were on their way to North Africa. American and British troops were going to invade territory that before the war had been under French control. By now, however, France had surrendered to Germany, and German troops had occupied much of North Africa. Even the French troops in North Africa were pledged to fight against the Allies should they invade the territory.

The landing was set for the morning of November 8, 1942. The evening before, religious services were held on the ship. Most of the nurses attended, along with the soldiers. Afterward there was little sleep. Instead the nurses talked and made jokes and wrote letters home, and pretended not to be afraid of what the morning might bring.

Shortly before dawn the Allied fleet began to bombard the shore. The entire ship shuddered as her big guns fired. All around, invisible except for the flash of the guns, other ships were firing. Watching from portholes and from sheltered spots on the deck, the nurses could sometimes see the huge shells glowing red as they passed through the air. They could see the distant explosions, like sheet lightning on the horizon.

The air turned gray with dawn. Through the mist the surrounding ships began to take shape. And now the sea was filled with small boats. They swarmed alongside the big ones. Soldiers went over the sides of the big ships and down ladders into the small ones. The small craft moved off toward the shore in long lines while the big guns of the fleet continued to fire over their heads. The nurses aboard the transports could not see any answering fire from the shore.

Lieutenant Phyllis MacDonald wrote to another nurse back in the States:

The firing was so intense that the ship rocked. We were all in an agony of suspense because no one seemed to know how our boys were doing. Then quite suddenly at 11 a.m. all sounds ceased and a great silence fell over the entire fleet. We

could still see smoke curling from the beach. It looked ghostly in the silence. Gradually word got around that the attack was successful and we were to prepare to land.

You should have seen us when we got dressed. We had on navy slacks, uniform blouse, helmet, gas mask, canteen belt, life preserver, and musette bag on our backs and our overcoats over our arms. We were going in small boats and we were told to leave everything unfastened, even our shoes untied, in case the boats got sunk and we had to swim. Of course there were some of us who couldn't swim....

A ship's ladder—actually a kind of stairway—hung over the side of the vessel. One after another the girls filed down it. Below them the small landing craft rose and fell with the waves. An officer at the foot of the ladder told each nurse, "Don't jump when the landing craft is going down with the wave. You might break an ankle. Wait until the boat comes up on the crest, then quick."

A few nights before, Ruth Haskell had fallen while getting out of her bunk during a storm. She had hurt her back, but she had said nothing about it because she was afraid she might not be allowed to land with the others. Now she looked at the small boat below her. It would rise almost level with the ship's ladder, then suddenly drop six feet, and rise again.

If she made a mistake here…

She watched the boat rise. The officer beside her said, "Now!" and she jumped. She hit the deck, stumbled, and someone caught her. There was a small pain in her back, but it was not bad.

Two or three doctors, five or six nurses, and ten to twenty corpsmen went in each boat. As Ruth's boat pulled away she looked back at the big ship. On the deck were two officers she had overheard talking the night before. They had been saying women had no place in a war; it was a mistake to bring nurses into a combat zone. "As soon as the going gets rough," one of them had said, "these girls are going to be more hindrance than help." But watching the nurses jump into the landing craft the officer had apparently changed his mind. When he saw Ruth looking at him he squared his shoulders and saluted, as one soldier to another.

The landing craft could not quite make the beach. The nurses, slacks rolled above their knees, had to go over the side, sometimes into waist-deep water. Then they floundered through the waves toward the shore. Corpsmen and doctors picked up some of the smaller women and carried them in. In her letter Lieutenant MacDonald wrote: "I staggered up on the beach and when I looked back and saw some of the other women being carried, legs dangling against some man's chest, I collapsed in laughter...as they were being dumped unceremoniously in the sand."

On shore, the nurses learned that their unit was to spend the night in two abandoned beach houses. Both houses had been partially destroyed by the Allied shellfire and were incredibly dirty. There could be no lights because snipers still roamed the area. The nurses ate some of the canned rations that each one carried in her musette bag; they drank water from their canteens. Because their bedrolls had not arrived, they lay down on the bare floor, covered only by their overcoats.

Ruth Haskell had just begun to doze uncomfortably when she heard Chief Nurse Archard calling, "Haskell, you and Atkins and Kelly. Report to headquarters. Wear full equipment."

Headquarters was the other beach house. Groping their way through the darkness the nurses found the Chief Surgeon in a dimly lit, blacked-out room. He told them that the Americans had taken over an old French-and-Arab hospital in the little town of Arzew. Casualties were already arriving and doctors, nurses, and corpsmen were needed. "You will go with Captains Borgmyer and Markham," he said.

Ruth Haskell would never forget the hours that followed.

First there was a long walk through the darkness. She did not know what direction they were going or who was leading the way. At last they reached a road where there were several parked jeeps. Ruth climbed into one, along with another nurse, a doctor, and a corpsman. A soldier was driving. Two soldiers, carrying machine guns, rode on the fenders. Traveling without lights, the jeeps started down the road.

They had been riding for about ten minutes when Ruth heard something whisk past her head. At the same instant there was a sharp crack from a rifle. "What...?"

"Sniper," a soldier whispered. The jeep kept going.

Houses loomed dark alongside the road. The little procession wound between them until it reached what seemed to be a town square. On one side a three-story building rose black against the sky. No lights showed anywhere. The jeep driver spoke to a soldier on guard. The guard answered, then turned and shouted for someone inside the building to put out the lights.

"This way," the guard said. A door opened. Ruth Haskell, with the other nurses, the doctors, and the corpsmen, passed through it.

She could see nothing, but the smell struck her like a blow. It was like something solid, alive, trying to choke her.

Mingled with it was the odor of ether and blood and indescribable filth. It made her take a half step backward. Then someone turned on a flashlight. The light slashed a narrow tunnel through the darkness—and she saw that men lay sprawled everywhere around her. Pale-faced, bloodstained, some motionless, some moving faintly, moaning or silent, they covered the floor. Some wore the uniforms of the French army, some were Americans, some Arabs. That much she could tell in the first instant.

"This way," a man said.

They were all using flashlights now, picking their way carefully past the men on the floor. A hand reached up and touched the bottom of Ruth Haskell's slacks. An American voice said, "A drink of water?"

She knelt beside him, raising his head carefully, giving him water from her canteen. When he had drunk she said, "Where are you hurt, soldier?"

The man gasped. "A woman!" he said in a half whisper. "An American woman! Where did you come from?"

"I'm a nurse," she said. "And we have doctors here now. We'll look after you."

Later, back in the States, Ruth Haskell would write a book about her experiences. In it she would say, "There has never been a time in my life that I was so proud to be a nurse, to be able to help."

There was much need for help. The hospital was old and decaying. Artillery fire had knocked out the few facilities it did have. In the operating room there was a bare table, one pale overhead light, a sink with a faucet from which the water would barely dribble. There were no operating gowns for doctors or nurses, no gloves, no time even to worry about such things. Haskell administered ether while her friend Kelly sterilized instruments over a single alcohol burner. Corpsmen brought in the patients one after another. There was no way to keep track of number or time.

The small overhead light blinked out. A corpsman moved close to hold two flashlights and the doctors kept working.

After a while the light came back on.

Another patient was ready to be brought into the room. Lieutenant Edna Atkins moved carefully beside him, holding a bottle of plasma. When the door opened to admit them, a draft blew the blackout curtain at the window. Outside, a rifle cracked sharply. A bullet ripped through the curtain over Haskell's head, past a doctor, and smashed into the wall. "Sniper!" a corpsman said, snatching the blackout curtain back into place.

Later in the night the same thing happened again. Then again. Without looking up from his work a doctor said, "I wish somebody would get that guy."

As if in answer there was the sharp chatter of a machine gun, followed by a thudding noise. Outside the building a voice shouted, "He was up in a tree. But you won't have to worry about him anymore."

All night the work went on, and all morning. About noon the other nurses arrived. Haskell, Atkins, and Kelly collapsed on bare cots and went to sleep.

For the others, the work went on. In a letter to her friend back home, Phyllis MacDonald wrote:

The next three days were a nightmare. Snipers still running wild and wounded were just being brought in from the surrounding villages. We had no water to wash with, just a little to drink, ate canned rations with no way to heat them. I was on night duty and our bedrolls hadn't arrived, so we had to lie on a plain cot, fully clothed, and try to sleep with a million flies buzzing around our heads and all that noise going on in the yard.

Sometimes it was funny. You would see someone going about, tending to his own business, and then suddenly he would start to run for dear life into the nearest foxhole or open doorway. Then the whizzing of the sniper's bullet would zing through the air. One of the girls was sick from all the cold rations and during one of her attacks she was vomiting and I was holding the basin for her while trying to keep one eye on what was going on.

The night of the third day our bedrolls came. We were allowed a helmet full of hot water, and sitting on those bare cots in dirty barracks with flies trying to eat us alive, we took our first bath and changed our clothes. Then for our own morale as well as that of the patients we combed our hair and put on some makeup, and breathed as though we had died and just returned to life.

By this time we heard rumors that the sniping was over and that hot food was to be had for supper. Honestly, Binny, when I stood in that chowline and smelled those weiners and sauerkraut and heard the good war news on the radio, a lump the size of an egg came in my throat and I had the most insane desire to cry, I was so happy. From then on we began to get our supplies; the boys weren't too bad that we were getting, and everything seemed a million times brighter.

The fighting ended around Arzew. But as the Allied invasion forces pressed inland, new battles were soon raging through the hill and desert country to the east. This was warfare of a kind never quite seen before. Highly mobile units of tanks and armored cars clashed in the open country like ships at sea. Frequently there was no established front line. The fighting moved swiftly forward—and just as swiftly back again.

Wherever it went, the 48th Surgical and other medical units went with it. They traveled in trucks, carrying their equipment with them. Operating tents and ward tents could be set up within a few hours. The nurses, doctors, and corpsmen slept in tents—and sometimes on the bare ground until there was time to put the tents up. Casualties from a battle would pour in and work would go on, hour after hour.

As soon as possible the patients were moved from the advance hospitals to safer and larger ones in the rear. Then the advance units might have a few days of rest. The nurses could visit nearby cities to go sightseeing or shopping in the ancient Arab bazaars, where the locals were friendly.

Once Phyllis MacDonald wrote to her friend:

You'll never guess where I just returned from. You know we've been taking canary baths out of basins, buckets, and even helmets. But in this place I visited there is an old original Roman bath. You go in this dilapidated building; it's very dark inside and after feeling your way around you see about six little cubby holes with a wooden bench and a few pegs up on the wall, apparently a recent addition. Then comes the great plunge. You walk in the next partition and down four stone steps into a bath that looks as big as a swimming pool. The water gushes out, nice and warm, from a big faucet. Two girls to a tub, and then you start soaking off dirt layer by layer. It was the most heavenly feeling. Just imagine not seeing a tub in four months and you can know what I mean.

Unfortunately, these periods of quiet never lasted long. Orders would come to move—and more than once that move had to be done in a rush to escape the advancing Germans. Once Theresa Archard was returning by car with two soldiers from a visit to a nearby city. She was afraid they might have lost their way. The hospital, which had been set up in the desert, had disappeared. They drove on, looking for it. In the darkness they actually passed beyond some of the advancing Germans' tanks, but managed to turn around and escape without being seen.

Then in May, 1943, six months after the invasion, the fighting in North Africa ended. The Allies had won there. Orders came to the advance hospitals to evacuate their patients and close down. Now the medical units would go into camp somewhere and have a long rest—or so they thought.

Already, however, new invasions and new battles were imminent. The medical units and their nurses would go where they were needed to care for the sick, the wounded, and the dying.

ITALY
CHAPTER FIVE

As is usually true in military operations, not all the medical units in North Africa lived under equally difficult conditions. Some were stationed well behind the front where there was little danger and working hours could be fairly regular. Often the nurses had ample time to go swimming in the Mediterranean, dancing at the officers' clubs, and shopping in the bazaars.

So it was with the 95th Evacuation Hospital—for a while. Its men and women lived quite pleasantly at a place called Ain El Turck in Algeria. "Our stay here," says the official hospital history, "bore all the earmarks of a summer vacation. We were established in a wheat field, but the site was a bare 300 yards from a lovely beach on the Mediterranean. Cool sea breezes tempered the hot days of July and August, and the opportunity to take a daily dip in the sea was taken advantage of by everyone."

Then, quite suddenly, came the new orders. All patients were to be sent elsewhere. The hospital was to close and prepare to move. No one knew just where, but everyone had an idea: Italy was to be invaded.

In September the men of the 95th went on board one ship, the nurses on another. The ships weighed anchor, joined convoys, and started north across the Mediterranean.

D-day for the Italian invasion was September 9, 1943. At noon that day the doctors and corpsmen of the 95th waded ashore not far from Salerno. The nurses were aboard the British hospital ship *Newfoundland*, scheduled to land the next day.

During the night the ship stayed well outside Salerno harbor. The rows of green lights around its hull glowed brightly in the darkness. Spotlights shone on the huge red crosses painted on the ship's funnel. As the nurses' history would say later, the ship was "lit up like a Christmas tree." The nurses slept soundly, sure that any passing German plane would respect the Geneva Convention that made hospitals and hospital ships safe from attack.

At five A.M. it was still dark. Out of the darkness a German plane struck without warning. Its bomb smashed squarely into *Newfoundland*.

Nurses were thrown from their bunks. The ship's lights were knocked out. In absolute darkness the women groped for flashlights they could not find. Everything was confused. Bunks had been torn from the bulkheads. Furniture lay scattered about the cabins.

Then the darkness was touched by red and yellow lights. The ship was afire.

Six of the British nurses also aboard *Newfoundland* had been killed. Three of the American nurses were wounded. Yet there was no panic. Swiftly they pulled on slacks, sweaters, and life jackets. Over the public-address system came orders to report to the lifeboats. Groping their way along dark passages, thankful now for the drills that had taught them exactly where to go, the women made their way to the lifeboats. The boats were lowered over the side. In the gray light of dawn the boats pulled away from the burning ship.

Another British ship, *St. Andrew*, picked up the nurses and took them back to North Africa. There the wounded were treated, the others given a brief rest.

Meanwhile the doctors and corpsmen of the 95th had set up their hospital close behind the fighting lines. Swamped with patients, they had a chance to realize how important nurses are in the care of the wounded. On September 13 the official hospital diary noted, "The fact our nurses are not with us is costly." And two days later, "The fact our nurses are not with us has proved a serious handicap to our medical and surgical staffs."

The nurses themselves did not have long to rest. Two weeks after the bombing of *Newfoundland* they waded ashore in Italy and rejoined the 95th.

Slowly, bloodily, American troops pushed up the Italian peninsula. The hospital units followed close behind. Sometimes they were so close to the fighting that their own artillery fired over their heads. The enemy artillery fired back, and more than once German shells fell into a hospital area. The nurses learned to tell the sound of the German shells from that of their own. At the first thin, keening whistle of a shell one might ask, "Ours?" Another would reply, "Theirs!" And all would dive for the nearest foxhole, or lie flat on the muddy ground beneath their cots.

Shelling was particularly heavy one night near the 11th Field Hospital. But battle casualties were being brought in at the same time, and in the receiving ward and operating tents the work went steadily on. Now and then a shell hit so close that the concussion knocked out the electric lights. Flashlights went on, emergency lanterns were lit. Lieutenant Betty Cook, from Kentucky, was wounded in the left arm. But it was not a serious wound, and another nurse applied a bandage.

In one of the wards Nurse Wilma Barnes, from Abilene, Texas, was giving a blood transfusion to a soldier named Clarence. Clarence was also from Texas, and Wilma had made a special favorite of him. Each time she heard the wail of an approaching shell she would say quickly, "You lie real still, Clarence," and hit the floor beside his cot, her hand still touching his arm. Then the shell would explode and Wilma would be on her feet again, holding the plasma bottle, making sure the needle was still in the vein.

A photographer, Margaret Bourke-White, visited the Italian front and later wrote a book about what she had seen. In it she said, "The nurses had learned how to build small dams and mudbanks to keep their tents from flooding in the rain. They knew how to tighten their tent pegs to keep their shelters from sailing away in the wind storms, and how to loosen their tent ropes again when the tentage dried out in the sun and shrank." She added, "They had raised the process of bathing in a helmet to a high science."

Chief Nurse Hallie Almond at the 38th Evacuation Hospital told Miss Bourke-White that the nurses sometimes became so exhausted they broke into tears. "Fatigue neurosis," she called it. And added, "But they only cry when their work is lightest. The minute we get a flow of badly wounded patients they are back on their feet, smiling and telling little jokes to make the boys feel better."

Of all the medical units involved in the Italian fighting, those on the Anzio beachhead suffered the most casualties.

At Anzio, American and British troops, brought by sea, were landed behind the German lines that stretched across Italy. The idea was to force those Germans fighting farther inland to retreat or be surrounded. But instead of retreating the Germans brought up large numbers of reserves. With tanks and artillery they smashed back at the invading Allies. The British and Americans found themselves confined to a narrow strip of land about fifteen miles long and no more than seven miles deep, every foot of which could be brought under fire by the German artillery.

This was the situation in which the army set up its field hospitals. They were, as the Medical Department history put it, "part of a front that had no back."

The hospitals, at first, were established in a park near the beach. It was a very pretty spot, with large shade trees and graceful buildings. The buildings were quickly marked

with huge red crosses, and the Germans did not shell them—intentionally. What happened unintentionally was something else.

The park was surrounded on all sides by legitimate targets. On the beach nearby, ships were unloading. There were fuel dumps on one side and ammunition dumps on another, and troops and trucks passing everywhere. On the first full day ashore Sergeant Louis Bliss, a corpsman working in the receiving ward, was wounded in the head by a shell fragment to become the first casualty. Another day there were twenty separate mass air attacks on the beachhead. These continued all day and all night. Some bombs fell in the hospital area, smashing buildings and wounding more personnel.

Something had to be done. Six days after the landing a decision was made to move the hospitals away from the park. The question was: where to move them? Since the beachhead was hemmed in on all sides, there was little choice. Finally, tents were set up in an open field. Here they were in full view of German artillery massed on hills only a few miles away. Indeed, they were close enough to hear the rattle of machine-gun fire and watch the tracer bullets streaking back and forth. But they were a little farther from their own fighting men and, therefore, less likely to be hit by mistake.

On the other hand, the tents offered no protection at all when a bomb or shell did fall in the area. It was impossible to dig deep foxholes: the hospitals were close to a swamp and holes more than one or two feet deep were apt to turn into wells. Although sand bags were piled around the edges of the tents, many of the wounded complained that they had felt safer in the front lines than they did in the hospitals.

Wind and rainstorms often lashed the area. They filled the shallow foxholes with water and turned the floors of the tents into deep mud.

These were the conditions under which the nurses had to work. And there was a tremendous amount of work. The fighting around the beachhead was some of the fiercest of the war. Casualties were brought in day and night. In the operating tents, doctors, nurses, and corpsmen worked until they staggered from weariness. Then new teams would replace them and the work would go on.

With new casualties constantly arriving, the wounded had to be transferred as quickly as possible. At night, long lines of ambulances would move from the hospitals to the

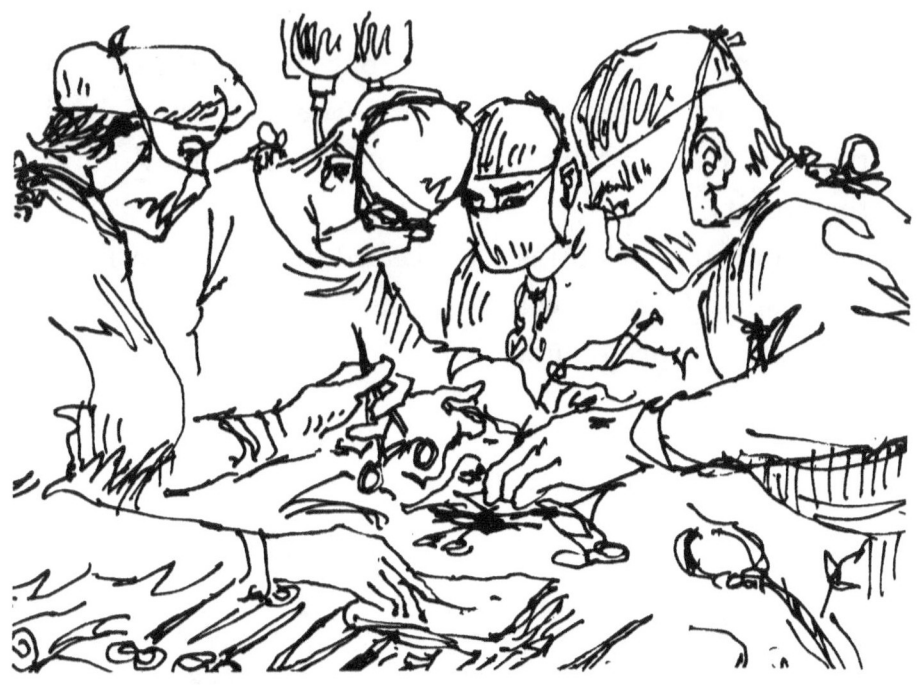

beach. The wounded would be put in small boats and carried to waiting hospital ships. One British hospital ship, the *St. David*, was bombed and sunk, even though brightly lighted. Two American nurses on board, Ruth Hindman and Anna Bess Berrett, were rescued; but two American medics, along with a number of the British, were lost.

Then came the afternoon of February 7. An air raid was going on, but air raids were so common that no one paid more than the normal amount of attention. In a ward tent of the 95th Evacuation Hospital, which had moved here after the fighting at Salerno, Lieutenant Marjorie Morrow was giving a blood transfusion to a badly wounded soldier. Chief Nurse Blanche Sigman and her assistant Carrie Sheetz, passing through the ward, stopped to help. As the three of them bent over the soldier's cot they could hear the steady thunder of antiaircraft guns from the beach, the roar of airplane engines, and the soft, frightening sound of shrapnel falling close around. Carefully, precisely, they went on with their work.

A corpsman from one of the other hospital units saw the German plane. It came from the direction of the harbor, very fast, with two British Spitfires close behind. The German pilot zigzagged violently to right and left, but the British fighters kept closing. In an effort to get more speed the German dumped the five bombs he was carrying.

All five fell among the tents of the 95th Evacuation Hospital. Blanche Sigman, Carrie Sheetz, and Marjorie Morrow, standing beside the cot of the wounded soldier, were killed instantly. (Later an army hospital ship would be named in honor of Chief Nurse Sigman.) Ruth Buckley and Fern Wingerd, working in another ward, were seriously wounded. In a matter of seconds sixteen persons, including doctors, nurses, corpsmen, and patients, were killed; sixty-four were wounded. Wards and operating tents were shattered, falling on the helpless patients within. Some of the tents caught fire.

It was a situation in which any man or woman might have panicked. Terror and shock were inevitable. And yet the uninjured nurses, most of them knocked down by the blast, got up and went swiftly to work. Along with uninjured corpsmen they tore the wrecked and burning tents away from the wounded. They found most of their supplies smashed, their operating tent blown apart. But from all over the hospital area help was coming. Every nurse, doctor, and corpsman who was off duty came running. Many of them worked the clock around, without relief.

Because so many of the 95th's key personnel were lost in the bombing, and so much of its equipment destroyed, another hospital unit was brought in to replace them. On the afternoon of February 10, the nurses of the 95th climbed into open trucks and started down what was called Purple Heart Drive—the short road leading to the docks. A storm was blowing and for several hours they could not board the ship waiting for them. While they waited,

"Whistling Willie," a long-range German cannon, began to shell the area. Luckily, none of the nurses were hit. Shortly after dark they were able to go aboard their ship.

Even as the nurses of the 95th Evacuation Hospital headed toward the open sea and safety, German artillery began to shell the hospital area they had left. Whether it was done deliberately or not, no one could say. It was dark, the storm was still blowing, and new casualties were being brought in from the front. In the operating tent of the 33rd Field Hospital, where Mary Roberts from Texas was acting Chief Nurse, three operating tables were filled. There came the sudden whine of a shell, and in almost the same instant the crash of its explosion.

A nurse gasped. "That sounded as if it was in our area."

"It was," one of the corpsmen said.

Then the second shell hit. It struck the generator just outside the operating tent. There was a great flash of fire and the lights went out.

The concussion had knocked Mary Roberts off her feet. For a minute she did not know whether or not she was wounded. Somewhere she heard a man moan. Then a doctor said, "We've got to have light in here," and the nurse stood up, groping through the darkness until she found one of the emergency lanterns and lit it.

Two of the corpsmen were on the ground, wounded, but the operating tables were still standing. Quickly Mary Roberts gave the lantern to one of the other corpsmen. She helped another nurse to her feet, speaking briskly to her and to another who stood as if frozen. She forced them and the unwounded corpsmen to go back to their jobs, then turned to the wounded. Shells were still falling, but inside the operating tent the work continued.

Some of the shells started fires, and the roaring wind spread the fires despite the rain. Within moments the area of the 33rd Field Hospital had turned into something out of a nightmare. In the stormy darkness the red and yellow flames seemed to light the sky but not the earth. One side of a tent would be bright with fire, the other inky dark. In the darkness the cries of the wounded, trapped in the burning tents, mingled with the roar of the storm. The operating tent itself caught fire. A nurse and corpsman started to bolt, but stopped when they saw Mary Roberts calmly carrying on with her job.

From all over the hospital area nurses, doctors, and corpsmen raced toward the 33rd Field Hospital section even though shells were still falling. They fought the fires, removed the wounded from the burning tents, and gave emergency treatment. After thirty minutes the shelling quit. Gradually the fires were brought under control.

Daylight found the 33rd a badly battered unit. Two nurses—Chief Nurse Glenda Spelhaug and 2nd Lieutenant LaVerne Farquhar—had been killed, another wounded. One corpsman had been killed, four doctors and seven corpsmen wounded. But the hospital was still functioning.

For their courage and gallantry in action that night three nurses—Mary Roberts, Elaine R. Roe of Whitewater,

Wisconsin, and Virginia Rourke of Chicago were given Silver Star medals. They were the first Silver Stars ever given to women in the history of the United States Army. The citations stated that the nurses' "exceptional coolness and outstanding leadership...bravery and complete disregard for personal welfare were in the finest tradition of the United States Army and Army Nurse Corps."

For four months the fierce fighting around the Anzio beachhead continued. In all that time there was no letup. There was no chance for rest or recreation. Once a group of off-duty doctors and corpsmen did try to start a ball game and some of the nurses went to watch. But German artillerymen on the nearby hills saw the crowd gathering. Perhaps they mistook it for a troop movement. Anyway, they began to shell the area and that was the end of the ball game. It was also the end of any crowds gathering in the open.

In May, Allied troops finally broke out of the beachhead and the fighting moved away from Anzio. Later an official army historian would sum up the role played by nurses in the victory:

In bitter front-line hours, the expression was commonly heard, "Well, if the nurses can take it, so can we." The knowledge that they stood as the only line of protection between the enemy and our medical installations on the beachhead strengthened the determination of countless Allied soldiers to fight the enemy with every ounce of energy they could muster....

In a situation as critical as that which developed on the beachhead—when subjective factors determined whether a line would hold or crack—the nurses assumed a major symbolic importance....

No enumeration of the elusive factors which enabled our men to hold their ground at Anzio can overlook the role played by the nurses there. Certainly no combat troops who were at Anzio will fail to honor those heroic women, six of whom lie buried side by side with infantrymen, tank drivers, artillery men, and others in the American cemetery on the beachhead.

TRAINING FOR WAR
CHAPTER SIX

Even before the first bombs fell on Pearl Harbor, some authorities were aware that if the United States went to war there would be a critical shortage of nurses. Many nursing schools were still suffering from the financial depression of the 1930s. Staffs were small and facilities limited. In 1940 and again in 1941 Congress appropriated small sums of money to help nursing schools, but the improvement was slight.

Then the bombs fell, and all over the country patriotic nurses left their civilian jobs to join the army and navy. This left the civilian hospitals desperately shorthanded. At the same time even more nurses were needed in the armed services. Indeed, the need was so great that at first no special military training was given the nurses who joined the service. There simply wasn't time. Also, few people thought—at first—that nurses would enter actual combat zones.

Bataan, Corregidor, North Africa soon proved that in modern war and modern medicine there is a need for nurses close to the front. Military training would be helpful, even for a nurse who already had her R.N.

To meet these demands the government began a double-barreled program. First, to get more people to go into nursing, a United States Cadet Nursing Corps was established. All over the country, nursing schools were enlarged with government money. Newspapers and magazines carried ads asking women to ENLIST IN A PROUD PROFESSION! TRAIN AS A NURSE! After her training, a Cadet Nurse could look forward to receiving an army or navy commission, as well as a Registered Nurse degree.

Within one year 65,000 women had joined the Cadet Nursing Corps. They were given tuition, books, room and board, and a small salary. Also, each woman was given indoor uniforms, plus one winter and two summer outdoor uniforms. The indoor uniforms were worn only in the hospital.

The winter uniform was a skirt and jacket of light gray flannel with silver buttons. On the sleeve was a silver Maltese Cross inside a scarlet oval. There were scarlet epaulets on the shoulders. The hat was a gray felt beret with the silver insignia of the U.S. Public Health Service on it. Over one shoulder hung a matching bag. The summer uniform was similar, but made of gray-and-white striped cotton.

On her scarlet epaulets a Cadet Nurse wore one silver Maltese Cross for each year of training. Each arm of this cross has two points so that from a distance it looks very much like a star, the insignia worn by generals and admirals. One day Cadet Martha Halfpenny was walking down a street in New Brunswick, New Jersey, proud of the second Maltese Cross which had just been added to her winter uniform. Two GIs standing on the corner watched her as she came near.

Suddenly the soldiers' eyes began to bulge. They snapped to attention, saluted, and stood rigid until she had passed. Then she heard one of them whisper to the other, "Who—who was that?"

"I don't know," the other said. "But she's a two-star general! I saw 'em on her shoulder!"

The second barrel of the government's nursing program was for the women who were already Registered Nurses. No longer did a nurse merely raise her right hand, take the oath, and next day find herself at work in a military hospital or on her way to the front. Instead, she was given a month or six weeks of basic training. Much of it was like the training any male GI might get—and the results were sometimes amusing as well as effective.

Take the case of Marie Pirl from Duquesne, Pennsylvania, who had never been outside her home state. She was deeply impressed with the necessity of obeying military orders to the letter. Her orders said to report to the

Commanding Officer, Fort Story, Virginia Beach, on or before January 11. She caught a bus that would get her there in plenty of time. Unfortunately she rode the bus straight past the camp without realizing it, and had to take another bus back. It was eleven p.m. when she arrived.

The Duty Officer at the gate checked Marie in, assured her she was on time, and told her to go to the Nurses' Quarters for the night. No, she said, she wanted to see the Commanding Officer. The Duty Officer, puzzled, asked why. "My orders said to report to him," Marie said.

Smiling, the officer explained this was merely military terminology. All orders read that way. She had checked in at the camp; that was all that was necessary.

Marie she stood her ground. "I was ordered to report to the Commanding Officer on the eleventh. I only have another half hour, and I want to report."

Finally the officer called a soldier. "Take her by the colonel's home," he said. "Then—if he doesn't eat her alive—take her to the Nurses' Quarters."

The colonel came to his door wearing pajamas and a robe. Obviously he had talked with the Duty Officer on the telephone because his face was twisted into what was half snarl and half grin. For a moment he looked at the nurse standing at attention on his front porch. "How old are you?" he asked.

"Twenty-one, sir."

His grin got the better of his snarl. "You look about fifteen. Anyway, you are too young to go around waking colonels in the middle of the night. Now you've reported, go on to the Nurses' Quarters where you belong."

The days that followed were equally filled with orderly confusion. On her first morning in camp Marie, along with other new nurses, was sent to a clothing warehouse. Here she was issued white working uniforms and oxfords. The outdoor uniform was a well-tailored olive drab with cap to match, tan shirts, ties, muffler, overcoat, rain coat, and brown oxfords. There were coveralls that seemed funny to the new nurses even though they fit, or almost fit—not like the men's coveralls that the nurses on Bataan and in North Africa had worn. There were ankle-high field-duty shoes that didn't need two or three pairs of heavy socks to make them fit. (Later, in New Guinea and the Philippines, Marie would wish she had more like them.)

Once the nurses were outfitted, the actual training began. There were lectures on the military ways of nursing. In the service with its rapid turnover of patients—and sometimes the need to pick up an entire hospital, move it, and set it up again in a hurry—things had to be done in a special way. There were lectures and training films on military courtesy, discipline, the safeguarding of military information, on tropical diseases, treatment of shock, and a dozen other subjects.

When the nurses were not going to lectures they were taking physical training, much of which was the same for them as for soldiers. The nurses learned to march for miles, carrying heavy packs. They learned to set up and take down tents. They had to run obstacle courses over high fences, under barbed wire, across wide ditches filled with muddy water. They had to crawl across a field under tangled barbed wire while machine guns fired live ammunition close overhead. They had abandon-ship drills. If there was no ship to practice on, they had to climb a rope ladder up one side of a high wall and down the other.

This physical training was far more difficult for some of the older nurses than for the younger ones. At one time the need for nurses was so acute that the army raised its age limit to forty-five. Bernice Tansy of Branford, New Hampshire, promptly joined. Despite being older than most of the nurses she held her own even in the judo classes and on the long, weary marches.

On most of these marches a regular drill sergeant was in command, but one day when the sergeant was not present Miss Tansy was told to drill the nurses. At first everything went perfectly. The nurses marched back and forth as precisely as a drill team.

Then it happened. The nurses were marching up a low hill on the left side of the road. Over the top of the hill came a platoon of soldiers jogging along in double time, heading straight for the nurses. Miss Tansy knew she should move the women to the right side of the road—but she couldn't think of the proper order. She couldn't think of any order at all. The soldiers kept jogging along and the nurses kept marching. It was a collision course.

At the last moment the officer in charge of the men shouted an order. The running column slanted to one side and past the nurses.

A year later, when Bernice Tansy and her nurses were almost trapped by German soldiers during the Battle of the Bulge, she would remember this incident. "I was a lot calmer trying to get away from the Germans," she would say later, "than I was trying to think of how to get those girls on the right side of the road."

And that was the purpose of the training.

ISLANDS OF THE PACIFIC
CHAPTER SEVEN

Edith Vowell, from Florida, joined the Army Nurse Corps shortly before the war began. She was stationed at Camp Davis in North Carolina. When a notice was posted asking for volunteers to go to the Philippines, she immediately went in to sign up.

"You are too late," the Chief Nurse told her. "Everybody here wants to get some of the luxury duty in the Philippines. We've had to close the lists."

Two months later the war started. Safe in North Carolina, Edith Vowell read the news stories about the fighting on Bataan. She wondered what would have happened to her had she reached the Chief Nurse's office a half hour earlier.

Her own orders for overseas duty arrived early in 1942. She was to report to the New York Port of Embarkation, and New York, Edith thought, meant she would be sent to England. However, when the convoy sailed no one could be sure where it was headed. Traveling a zigzag course to confuse prowling submarines, the ships sometimes seemed to be heading east, sometimes south.

Gradually the weather got warmer. Then one morning the convoy moved slowly toward land and began to pass through the Panama Canal. "Wherever we are going," one of the nurses said, "it won't be England."

It proved to be Brisbane, Australia. And, strangely enough, to Edith Vowell it seemed very much like home. Halfway around the world, it was just about as far south of the equator as her home in Florida was north of it. Bougainvillaea and poinsettias bloomed in the semitropical sun just as they had bloomed in her yard at home. The people were hospitable and friendly and they spoke English —even if they did have what sounded to Edith like a "foreign" accent.

At this time, in the spring of 1942, Japanese troops were still driving closer and closer to Australia. They had captured most of the East Indies. In the jungles of New Guinea they were pushing back the Australian and American forces under General Douglas MacArthur. Casualties—both wounded and diseased—were brought down to the Australian hospitals. After the great naval battle of the Coral Sea, wounded sailors and aviators began to arrive.

The 153rd Station Hospital, where Edith Vowell was located, was some sixty miles outside Brisbane in what had been a college. It was a pleasant place, and despite the work there was time for leisure and sightseeing. Then, suddenly, she and some of the other nurses received orders to pack and be ready to move. No one knew where.

This time it was the island of New Guinea, one of the most remote and unknown areas of the world. At Port Moresby the fighting was so close the nurses could often hear the guns booming in the mountains. Japanese bombers came over day and night. Even so, in New Guinea nature was a more persistent and terrible enemy than the Japanese.

There was one corrugated-iron building in the hospital camp. Here were placed the sickest patients and those with arms or legs in traction. Everyone else, including the nurses, lived and worked in tents, and sometimes in native grass huts. And there was rain. It fell in torrents, in solid sheets. To Edith Vowell it sometimes seemed as if she were

trying to live in the middle of a river that ran straight down from the sky instead of across the earth. The earth itself was a quagmire of sucking, sticky mud. During her first day in New Guinea, Edith changed her shoes five times, trying to dry one pair while she wore the other. After that she gave up and wore a pair of men's high-topped shoes with three pairs of socks to make them fit.

It was a land of sudden and savage changes. When the rain quit, the sun blazed down. The equator was only a few hundred miles to the north, and the heat was sometimes almost unbearable. Indeed, some of the nurses said this was the only country in the world where you could stand in mud up to your knees while your face was filled with dust. This dust was so fine that even a footstep could stir it like a small explosion. And army bulldozers were constantly building new roads, trucks were grinding back and forth over them, airplanes were landing and taking off from the nearby field—so that over everything hung a vast, thick, drifting cloud of dust.

And there were mosquitoes. Friendly airplanes roared back and forth spraying insecticides instead of bombs, but the mosquitoes persisted. They carried a variety of tropical diseases, of which the most feared was cerebral malaria. Soldiers brought to the hospital were as often diseased as wounded—and the mosquitoes would just as soon bite a nurse as a soldier. To prevent malaria the nurses had to take daily doses of Atabrine. This was worse on the blondes than on the brunettes, Edith Vowell thought. It made her hair an odd shade of yellow and her skin faintly green. On the other hand, the brunettes thought the drug was harder on them. It made their skin and the whites of their eyes the same pale "Atabrine yellow."

Sometimes, when the fighting to the north had been particularly heavy, the nurses worked the clock around. On the other hand, there was often time for leisure. Nurses went on mountain picnics with officers from the nearby airfield. They took jeeps to visit nearby rubber plantations and native villages with their thatched houses built on high stilts. They took walks through the jungle to where a mountain stream came crashing over a high and beautiful fall. The nights were often pleasantly cool, with a moon that seemed bigger and whiter and brighter than in any other part of the world. It was fine for romance, except that the Japanese often took advantage of the moonlight to send over bombing planes. Then a nurse and her date might have to share a foxhole until the raid was over.

Worse than the Japanese bombs—or so some of the nurses thought—were the spiders. One day, diving head first into a foxhole, Lieutenant Vowell found herself face to face with a giant, hairy-legged spider. Immediately she whirled and dived back into the open. "That spider looked a lot bigger and more deadly than any Japanese airplane," she explained later. "From that time on I carried a shovel with me when there was an air raid. It took something big as a shovel to swat a New Guinea spider."

Gradually MacArthur's soldiers pushed the Japanese northwestward along the coast of New Guinea. The field hospitals and evacuation hospitals followed closely. At the same time naval warfare was spreading through the South Pacific. Naval hospitals began to spring up on remote tropical islands whose names had scarcely been known to one American out of a hundred before the war began.

At New Caledonia the fleet hospital was built on a point of sandy beach. In front lay the harbor with its coral reef and blue sea just beyond. On the other three sides was

what had been the official garden of the French governor, with drives bordered by tall palms and wide lawns and formal gardens. The nurses lived in tents nearby, until the Seabees of the navy construction battalion could build quarters for them. Behind the quarters rose wooded mountains laced by clear, swift-running streams. Often these spilled over high falls, the water so white it looked like lacy scarfs blown in the wind. Trade winds kept temperatures mild.

New Caledonia had been under French control before the war. French officials and planters still lived in Noumea, the capital city, their homes half buried under great masses of red and purple and yellow flowers. Melanesians, Polynesians, Javanese and Tonkinese people mixed freely with American sailors, Seabees, marines, and airmen. With them the nurses went on beach picnics and swam in the glass-clear water. They learned to spear fish and bet on the crab races, the favorite sport of the marines. They climbed the mountains to visit the waterfalls and hunt the small, wild deer that seemed so out of place in this tropical setting.

Not all the Pacific Islands were as pleasant as New Caledonia. On many the weather was worse and the conveniences fewer. At Espiritu Santo the hospital was built in a coconut grove with no town of any kind nearby, not even a native village. At Efate the sun beat mercilessly down on the metal buildings. Guadalcanal and Tulagi were even worse. The places were alive with creeping, crawling, and flying creatures, from tiny copra bugs that clung to your skin and couldn't be brushed off, to big land crabs, sometimes so many that it was impossible to walk at night without stepping on them. When motion pictures were shown to the troops on outdoor screens, flying foxes—big batlike creatures—swooped across the screens. When the sun did not beat down, the rain fell in torrents and the nurses' clothing mildewed overnight. Rats invaded the quarters to gnaw at anything left unprotected.

To these hospitals were brought the casualties from naval battles and from land fighting in the Solomon Islands. Many of the wounded men, especially those from bombed and torpedoed ships, had been terribly burned, often about the face. With these disfigured men depression was sometimes worse than their wounds. Many of them felt they could never go home again, could never face their wives or sweethearts. One of the first things the nurses had to learn was to let no sign of shock or revulsion show on their own faces at the sight of a badly scarred patient. Instead, they learned to smile and calmly assure the man he was going to be all right. "Just wait," they often said. "When your girl back home sees you, you'll be more handsome than ever." And very often they were right because the doctors indeed did wonderful work.

The very fact that nurses were there and could smile at them was a great boost to the morale of these patients. The nurses learned too that one wounded man could sometimes cheer up another when nothing else would help. On Efate, Ensign Theresa Hayes noticed that one of her patients was very depressed. He was not more than twenty years old and had lost a leg when his ship was torpedoed. "It's your job to cheer me up," he told Theresa, "but you don't mean it. I know that a one-legged man can't be of much use to anybody."

Later Theresa spoke to another patient about the boy. This was an older man with both hands gone, his jaw shattered by a bomb and wired in place. "I think you could help that boy in the next ward," she said.

The man nodded. He went into the next ward and sat down on the side of the boy's bed. "Have you got a cigarette?" he asked. His voice was a kind of hiss, because of the wires holding his broken jaw in place.

"Sure," the boy said. He took one from the table beside his bed.

The man grinned as best he could. He held up his handless arms. "You'll have to light it—and hold it for me."

"Sure, sure," the boy said. And learning that he could do this—that some people were worse off than he was and that he could be of help to them—changed his attitude. From that time on he became more cheerful and began to recover.

On many of the islands the wards sometimes resembled pet shops as much as hospitals. Wherever there were soldiers and sailors there were almost certainly dogs, and sometimes cats. There were pet monkeys, pet parrots and parakeets, and sometimes strange birds most of the nurses had never even heard of before. On New Caledonia there was a bird, found nowhere else in the world, called a kagu. It couldn't fly, it wasn't pretty, and it made a noise like a dog's bark; but the nurses and the sailors loved it. On Efate there were even trained geckos—big, greenish lizards—and the patients made bets on which one could catch the most mosquitoes.

No matter where the nurses were located, no matter what conditions they had to live under, they tried to make their quarters comfortable and homelike. At Oro Bay on the northeast coast of New Guinea, where the nurses lived in thatched native huts with dirt floors, they made furniture out of old packing crates. They sewed curtains from bed sheets and even parachutes. They put up pictures, painting their own when necessary.

And everywhere they had gardens. Wherever the nurses were sent they took seeds and plants with them. They grew marigolds, bachelor buttons, and morning glories. On many of the islands tomatoes grew to surprising size. Nasturtiums were not only pretty to look at but their leaves could be used in place of lettuce in salads.

Advancing northward toward Japan, General MacArthur and his troops reinvaded the Philippines in October, 1944. Among the first nurses flown in to care for the casualties was Marie Pirl, the woman who had never been outside Pennsylvania until she joined the Army Nurse Corps. She had been stationed in the jungles of New Guinea, and now she took her flower and vegetable seeds with her. The evacuation hospital was so close to the front that Marie and the other nurses could see the flash of the guns. Sometimes the Japanese shelled the buildings; there were so many holes in the roof that on rainy days the operating tables had to be moved from place to place to dodge the leaks. Only emergency operations were performed here; as soon as possible, the wounded were sent to safer places in the rear.

Despite the shelling and the long hours of work, Lieutenant Pirl planted her garden. Before her tomatoes could ripen or her nasturtiums bloom, the fighting would move on and the hospital with it. That did not matter. What mattered was that a small bit of garden had helped the morale of everyone—doctors, nurses, corpsmen, and patients.

HOSPITAL SHIP
CHAPTER EIGHT

The nurses stood with their hands resting on the ship's rail. Except for their white uniforms and the quiet tenseness with which they waited, they might have been aboard a cruise ship looking across the gray water toward some foreign land. It was just dawn, on February 19, 1945. A mist hung over the sea. Above the mist the nurses could see the ragged crest of Mount Suribachi on Iwo Jima.

"Here they come," one of the nurses said. Her voice was barely audible and her hands were tight on the rail.

"Here they come." It was another voice, then another. "The boys are coming." The word passed swiftly through the ship. Doctors, corpsmen, the ship's crew, everyone who did not have to stay at an assigned post, moved toward the deck.

Now the landing barges could be seen looming out of the mist. But these barges were not heading toward the beach; they were coming from it, carrying the wounded. As they drew nearer, the nurses leaning over the rail could see the filthy, bandaged, bloodstained men. Some were standing; some sat with their backs against the bulkheads; some lay motionless, strapped onto dirty stretchers. The water was rough. Spray flew over the sides of the landing barges, soaking both the crews and the wounded.

Carefully the barges came alongside the great white ship with its green band and red crosses. In the pitching sea, stretchers were fastened to hoists and lifted aboard. Some of the wounded, able to walk, came up the gang plank without any help. Some had to be carried. The empty barges moved away and new barges took their place.

Doctors moved swiftly among the wounded. Tied to each man was a tag describing his injury and condition. The tags had been prepared at the first-aid station ashore. Now the ship's doctors looked quickly at the tags and at the wounded men. "Take him to surgery. Give him plasma." The corpsmen lifted the stretchers and moved away. The nurses went with them. The work had begun.

All day the wounded were brought aboard. Later a woman correspondent on one of the hospital ships wrote:

By nightfall the neat, shining white wards with their double-decked bunks were almost filled. On the once spotless white decks were little piles of dirty blood-stained clothing which had been cut off the men. The stain was everywhere—

a splash on the toe of my shoe, little droplets on the railing where I rested my hand. You fortify yourself against it in the operating rooms, train yourself to ignore it on bandages, on the doctors' white gowns. But there is no getting used to it everywhere.

With darkness the great white ship upped anchor and turned toward the open sea. Under international law a hospital ship must travel fully lighted. But if the lights had been turned on close to shore, surrounded by friendly warships, they would have exposed those ships to enemy guns and planes. So with darkness the hospital ship moved away from the beach, lit up, and cruised in circles.

In the operating rooms and almost-filled wards, the doctors and nurses worked all night. Usually the first thing a wounded man wanted, if he was still conscious, was to get his shoes off. It might be the first time he'd had them off in days or even weeks. Grimy, bloodstained clothing

had to be removed, baths given, wounds bandaged. The nurses gave morphine to relieve pain. They gave plasma to diminish shock and keep the patient alive until there was space in the operating rooms for him.

With dawn the hospital ship turned back toward Iwo Jima. Gradually the island loomed out of the mist, surrounded by an unbelievable forest of American warships. The white ship picked a way between them, drawing closer and closer to the island until even men running along the beach were visible. Then the anchor went down and the barges filled with wounded began to come alongside once more.

✚

One ship, the U.S.S. *Samaritan*, had been at anchor only a short time on its second day of loading wounded men when a shell struck. It ripped through the super structure, missed a nurse and corpsman by inches, tore through two decks and into a ventilator—and did not explode. By sheer luck no one was hurt. The ship's crew defused the shell and got it over the side. For the medical personnel there was scarcely time even to ask what had happened.

In all probability the Japanese gunners had not aimed at *Samaritan*. From the Japanese point of view there were bigger, more important targets all around her. The landing of a shell was simply one of the risks of war.

By afternoon of the second day all of *Samaritan*'s wards were filled. The ship's crew moved out of their quarters to make room for the wounded. Medical personnel slept on the deck, if they slept at all. There was simply not room for another patient. Yet the landing barges were still coming, each filled with its tragic burden.

Now the senior medical officer had to make the decision. From the ship's rail he could see the wounded lying quietly, patiently, in the barges, waiting to be brought on

board, waiting for the help that might mean life or death. But to take on more patients now would make it impossible to provide proper care for those already on board. The medical officer turned to the ship's captain. "We'd best head for Saipan, Captain."

"Very well."

The captain gave his orders. Over the bullhorn the word went out to the barges to stand off. The *Samaritan*'s anchor was coming up.

In one of the barges a bosun's mate began to scream curses. "You can't go now!" he shouted. "You've got to take these men on board! They're dying! You hear? You've got to take them!"

Both the captain and the senior medical officer could hear, but they had no choice. Their only consolation was the knowledge that another hospital ship would soon take their place.

At full speed *Samaritan* headed for Saipan and the land-based hospitals located there. One of the wounded men would later write a book about his experiences:

I wasn't doing any visiting around the ship but what I could see from my own bed was enough to demonstrate that this was no movie version of tender white hands, peace and beauty. The ship smelled of blood, vomit, corruption, and hot, feverish flesh. And the many voices of pain murmured always in the hot air....

In the four and a half days I spent in the Samaritan *the operating room lights never went out. By the time they discharged us at Saipan and turned back for another trip the surgeons and nurses and corpsmen were red-eyed with lack of sleep and staggering with weariness.... Yet the patience of the nurses and corpsmen was hard to believe.... In the time I spent with them I never heard a sharp or impatient word addressed to any patient.*

Of course life on a hospital ship was not always so hectic as during the time of a major invasion. Indeed, the nurses assigned to hospital ships were often referred to as the Belles of the Pacific, the women with the best duty in either the Army Nurse Corps or the Navy Nurse Corps. Between invasions there were times when work was light and the ships had few if any patients. Then whenever a hospital ship entered one of the great fleet anchorages such as Ulithi or Majuro, all the sailors in the harbor would rush to stare across the water at the women; or if they weren't visible, just to look at the ship that carried them. On every ship, blinker lights began to flash, with officers sending invitations for the nurses to come aboard for dinner. Often there would be some world-famous admiral or general aboard. Invitations would be flown in from remote, outlying islands, asking nurses to dances at officers' clubs that no woman had visited in weeks or months, or perhaps ever. Once or twice a week a special dinner would be given on the hospital ship, and the nurses could invite their newmade friends in return.

Leota Hurley, a good-humored woman whose friends called her Lee, joined the U.S.S. *Bountiful* at Ulithi in

the spring of 1945. She was one of a new group of nurses, replacing the veterans who had been aboard for the invasion of Saipan, Guam, Iwo Jima, and other islands. For a few days life seemed to be just one big party. Even when the *Bountiful* left the atoll, sailing northwest, there was little work. There were bandages to roll, applicators to get ready, abandon-ship drills now and then; but on the whole it seemed at first almost like a pleasure cruise. Then, talking with one of the doctors, Lee Hurley learned that she was supposed to be able to give intravenous injections. At this time many hospitals did not teach nurses to give such injections. Lee did not know how, nor did any of the other nurses on board. A number of the nurses crowded into Lee's small stateroom to discuss the matter. One of the main jobs of the military nurses was to train the corpsmen, many of whom had had no medical training before they joined the service. Yet on the *Bountiful* several of the corpsmen could give intravenous injections. "But we can't ask them to teach us," Lee said. "We are officers and they are enlisted men. We'd never be able to keep any discipline if we let them think they know more than we do."

"We can't ask the doctors," another girl said. "They think we already know."

"All right," Lee said. "We'll teach ourselves."

So for the next few days the girls secretly practiced on one another—putting a tourniquet around the upper arm so the vein in the inside of the elbow stood up clearly, then inserting a needle into the vein. This was the difficult part. Once a nurse had found the vein she would remove the needle and try it again. Then the other nurse would practice on her. It was a good thing they had long-sleeved uniforms because the arms of most of the nurses were soon badly discolored. But they had learned to give intravenous injections.

That skill was put to use very quickly to save lives. On April 1, 1945, American forces invaded the island of Okinawa, just 350 miles south of Japan itself. Offshore at Okinawa, the greatest fleet in the history of the world was under almost constant attack by Kamikazes, the Japanese suicide pilots who tried to sink American ships by deliberately crashing their planes into the ships. So both ashore and afloat the casualties were mounting. Here the *Bountiful* took on a load of patients. The new nurses worked hour after hour, day after day, injecting lifesaving plasma and antibiotics into the veins of the wounded men.

Once Lee Hurley was giving plasma to a wounded marine when, slowly, his eyes opened. For several moments the boy looked at her as though he could not believe what he saw. Probably the last thing he remembered was the impact of the bullet on Okinawa. Now a nurse in a white uniform was bending over him, her hand resting on his arm. "My," he whispered. "My, you're beautiful." And then, "Am I going to get well?"

"Of course you are." She smiled at him. He let out a long breath. "You're beautiful," he said again, and went to sleep.

Bountiful delivered her casualties to the base hospital at Ulithi, then turned back toward Okinawa for more wounded. This time she ran into a typhoon at night. Later Lee Hurley wrote to her family back in Vermont:

We finally decided to get up and get dressed. It was a riot trying to get dressed as we just could not stand still. Eating breakfast was just as impossible, our chairs sliding so much we had to hang on with one hand while eating with the other....

The storm grew in intensity until about 11 o'clock when it reached a climax. We really did get frightened then. We made a roll which was just about as bad as we could do and not tip.

You should have heard the noise. Everything that was not

fastened in place went crashing and rolling around. We seemed to be standing on our side for minutes. Everyone was hanging on to each other or something and wondering if we were really coming out of that roll. At the same time the wind blew our siren again. We thought we were really sinking....

The storm finally subsided.... We were happy and thankful, yet it was so unusual and exciting I would not have missed it for $1000.

It was a different and more tragic scene off Okinawa on the night of April 28. Overhead a full moon shone in a clear sky. The sea was calm and the hospital ship *Comfort* with all her lights burning, the great red crosses on her funnel showing clearly, looked very beautiful on the moonlit sea. On board, however, there was no time to enjoy the beauty. *Comfort*'s wards and operating rooms were crowded with wounded. Her doctors, nurses, and corpsmen worked steadily.

About 8:30 the crew of the ship heard an airplane. Moments later it passed overhead, so low that they could see the Japanese markings on the wings. No guns fired at it because *Comfort* carried no guns. The plane passed, circled, and started back.

In *Comfort*'s operating room no one heard the plane. The tables were filled with critically wounded. More wounded waited in the corridors and wards. The medical personnel worked on.

Standing in the bow, the ship's lookout watched the plane. It was coming faster now, in a long, shallow dive.

But it would simply pass close, the lookout thought. Then he knew better. He began to scream a warning. Seconds later the plane plunged head-on into the ship's superstructure. It tore through into the operating room and exploded.

Twenty-three persons, including six nurses, were killed; thirty-eight, including four nurses, were wounded. For a while fires threatened the entire ship. Gradually they were brought under control. *Comfort* limped on toward Saipan while those nurses still on their feet worked to save the new wounded as well as the old.

FLIGHT NURSE
CHAPTER NINE

In World War II, as in other wars, the life of a wounded man often depended on how quickly he got medical attention. Corpsmen followed the front-line troops straight into battle and brought the wounded back on stretchers to first-aid stations. Here the doctors worked, often under direct shellfire. But this was emergency treatment only. For the seriously wounded, hospital treatment was necessary, and time precious. The airplane was the obvious answer.

When the army and navy first began to evacuate their wounded by air, there were not enough doctors to put one on every plane. Doctors at the forward station would decide which patients should be flown out. Then a corpsman would be placed on the plane to attend to the wounded during the flight.

The corpsmen were brave. Some of the most heroic deeds in the war were performed by army and navy corpsmen who often risked their lives to save the wounded. But most of them had had very little medical training. A trained nurse plus a corpsman on each plane would be the answer—except for one thing.

The transport planes, after taking wounded away from the fighting, brought in supplies on their return. Therefore they could not be marked with red crosses. Without this symbol they were fair game for enemy gunners and fighter planes. Both the army and navy hesitated to send women on such dangerous missions.

It was the heroism of the nurses on Bataan and Corregidor that convinced the authorities. First the army, then the navy, set up flight schools to train nurses in aeromedicine. The authorities, explaining that flight nursing would be dangerous duty, asked for volunteers. So many nurses volunteered that only about one in five could be accepted.

At flight school the nurses were first put through an intensive period of study. They learned that the gas in a human being's stomach expands with altitude: at 15,000 feet its volume is twice what it would be at sea level; at 25,000 feet it is tripled. Therefore special care had to be given to patients with abdominal wounds; otherwise, sutures put in at the forward evacuation hospital might rupture. A lack of oxygen at high altitudes was particularly critical for patients with head and chest wounds. To help the nurses understand the effects of oxygen shortage, they

were put in decompression chambers. As the oxygen was withdrawn they could see how their fingernails turned blue, and how their thinking and coordination became fuzzy. They learned to use oxygen masks and study the effect of oxygen on themselves and on patients.

Along with their studies in aeromedicine, the nurses learned how to load and unload patients from an airplane. Since many of the flights would be over water, they learned how to inflate life rafts. They learned how to get the wounded as swiftly as possible out of a sinking plane and onto a raft. Also, each flight nurse had to be a good swimmer. The navy required each woman to be able to swim a mile by herself and to tow a victim for 220 yards.

The first nurse to land on Iwo Jima was 23-year-old Jane Kendeigh, whom the boys called "Candy." The battle was in full force when her transport plane arrived. Japanese guns were shelling the airfield, which had just been taken by the Americans. Japanese planes were bombing it, and American antiaircraft guns were firing at the Japanese planes. For more than an hour the slow, unarmed transport plane circled over the American ships offshore, while Jane

and the crew hoped no Japanese plane would jump it, and no American ship mistake it for an enemy aircraft. When the enemy planes finally turned back for Japan, the transport went in to land. But the Japanese guns, hidden on the surrounding hills, were still firing at it.

Later, when the transport was back in the air again, carrying its cargo of wounded, Candy told the corpsman working with her, "I don't remember being frightened while we were on the ground. There wasn't time to think about anything except getting these wounded men on board. But now we are safe, in the air again, I find my knees are shaking so I can hardly stand up."

From Iwo and Okinawa, the flight nurses and their patients were flown back to hospitals at Ulithi and Saipan and Guam. From there they might be flown to Pearl Harbor, and later still back to the United States. It was the same with the war in Europe. A flight nurse might be in France one day and New York the next. One week she might be dodging sniper fire on Guadalcanal, the next week dancing at the Officer's Club in Pearl Harbor or surfing at Waikiki—with no telling what adventures in between. For example, Lieutenant Dorothy Shikoski was injured when engine trouble forced her plane down at sea. But she stayed on the sinking plane until all the patients

were safely transferred to life rafts. Lieutenant Kathleen Dial won an Air Medal for a similar experience in the South Pacific.

The greatest adventure of them all, perhaps, was shared by Lieutenant Agnes Jensen, of Stanwood, Michigan, and twelve other nurses. It was one of the truly great adventures of the war and it happened this way.

Shortly after daylight on the morning of November 8, 1943, a transport plane took off from Catania, Sicily. On board were thirteen flight nurses, thirteen corpsmen, and the plane's crew of four. They were to fly to Bari, Italy, where the nurses and corpsmen would pick up planes loaded with wounded and return with them to the hospital in Sicily.

It was a gray morning with a thin mist of rain. This was supposed to clear up before they reached Bari; instead, the weather turned worse. Clouds enveloped the plane so that at times even the wingtips were invisible. In the rough air the plane bucked and pitched like a horse. Twice waterspouts loomed up ahead, but the plane dodged them.

Agnes Jensen had made this flight several times before. She knew that it usually took no more than two hours. Now after four hours the plane was still groping its way through heavy clouds. From where she sat in the second bucket seat on the starboard side, Lieutenant Jensen could watch the radio operator. He was working desperately with his set, checking and rechecking, but obviously something had gone wrong.

Eventually there was a break in the clouds and looking

down through it Agnes Jensen could see a small landing field. As the plane began to circle, Lieutenant James Baggs, the copilot, came back into the cabin. "We are going to try to land," he said. "It may be rough, so make sure your seat belts are fastened."

Agnes Jensen fastened her seat belt, then leaned to look out the window. The visibility was poor but she could see a few planes lined up alongside the field. Somehow they did not look like any planes she had seen before. Then, suddenly, she could see the German markings on the wings. At the same time guns began to fire. The transport jolted as it was hit somewhere near the tail.

Lieutenant Charles Thrasher, the pilot, gunned his engines and pulled back on the wheel. For a few seconds the plane seemed to be flying through a solid mass of bursting antiaircraft fire. Then it was hidden in the clouds again.

By now everyone on the plane knew they were not only lost, but somewhere behind the German lines. Also, they were low on gas. Once, through a break in the clouds, Agnes Jensen saw a mountain. It loomed out of the clouds below them, and into clouds above them. Had they been another mile to the west they would have crashed into it.

There were thirty persons aboard the plane. Agnes counted six Mae West life jackets swinging from a bulkhead in the stern. Only six, if they should come down at sea. She had already counted the parachutes on board. Six of them. So there would be no chance for all the passengers to bail out. And the gas was getting lower.

Later Agnes wrote to a friend:

I can remember cautiously glancing down the aisle at the nurses, trying to see their reactions (five of the thirteen were former stewardesses) but mostly they were a bunch of stoics. Perhaps our training accounted for it—nursing and airlines and air evacuation—for I could easily see that some of the sergeants across the aisle were frightened. Because of their apprehension I didn't want to appear too anxious about our situation. Nonetheless, as I saw it we had very slim chances and with these thoughts I started "writing off" all the passengers.

The nurses I knew fairly well. Two were married. I knew a few of the sergeants, but only by name. I sat and studied each one, wondering which might be married and perhaps leaving children as well. After having gone down the entire line and after checking us all off, I decided I didn't want to know when we hit that mountain.

So I fixed our musette bags in the front seat where I could put my head down. I must have dozed off, for I was rather startled when Thrasher came out and said there was a hole in the clouds with what looked like level ground below. He was going to try a wheels-up belly landing. He did put the wheels down, however, and it was wonderful those first seconds to feel them rolling under us. Then the wheels mired; the nose of the plane rooted into the mud, and boxes that had been piled in the rear of the plane were flying all over the place.

Luckily no one was seriously injured, and they all climbed out. They found they were standing in a cornfield in a driving rain. Mountains loomed dimly around them, but there were no houses and no people. Then, abruptly, men were running toward them from every direction. They were carrying guns, but they were not in German uniform. One of the strangers was riding a white horse. He stopped directly in front of Agnes Jensen, jumped off, and shook her hand. "Americano!" he said happily. "Americano!"

Gradually she understood that the plane had landed in Albania. Albania had been captured by the Germans, but these men were Partisan fighters, still carrying on guerrilla warfare against the Germans.

In her letter Agnes mentioned the Albanian leader:

He went on to welcome the others and I turned to go back in the plane and met Ann Maness, a tall girl from Texas, coming out. I stopped and must have stared at her, for my mind was whirling. All I could think was, Ann is here too! *Having "written off" all of us only a short while before it took me a while to think,* Oh, we've landed! We're safe!

German troops as well as the Albanian Partisans had heard the plane land. Hurriedly the Americans took what little food and medical supplies there were in the plane. The nurses grabbed their musette bags containing make-up, one extra shirt, underwear, and socks—the only extra clothing they had with them. Then the thirty Americans followed the Albanians through the rain into the mountains.

For two days they stayed hidden in a cottage that had a fireplace but no chimney, windows but no windowpanes, no tables, no chairs, and no bathroom. They slept on the floor around the fire. "Actually," Agnes Jensen said later, "it was a tossup as to whether we would rather freeze or be suffocated by the smoke."

The German troops were still looking for them and after two days they had to move. Albanian guides led them first to one small village, then to another. Wherever they went the people welcomed them. But these people were desperately poor. Agnes wrote:

We all picked up body lice from the local homes, and no wonder, for they would more often than not push over a goat or sheep to make room for us at the fireplace. Seldom did they have any cover to offer us. The Albanians had learned the hard way that when the Germans came they took all movable belongings, and often hostages. So any extra blankets, dishes, etc., had been carefully hidden.

Food was almost as scarce as blankets, and strange indeed to the Americans. Mostly it was beans and a kind of corn bread without salt. Sometimes there was goat-milk cheese, so strong that the nurses almost gagged on it. One by one most of the Americans became sick, but there was little chance to rest. No one village could feed all of them for long, and the Germans were always close behind.

Clothing began to wear out, particularly shoes. The sole of one of Agnes Jensen's shoes tore loose so that it flapped when she walked. Some of the Americans had no soles left at all.

Once German tanks and Partisan fighters battled on

the outskirts of a small village in which the Americans were staying. The Germans won. As their tanks came rumbling into the small town, almost everyone, Americans and Albanians, ran for the hills to hide. In the resulting confusion three of the nurses, Lieutenants Wilma Lytle, Ann Maness, and Helen Porter, disappeared. Had they been captured? Killed? No one knew. As the Americans—now ten nurses and seventeen men—continued their strange journey they often wondered what had happened to their friends.

A few British Secret Service men were working behind the German lines in Albania. Lieutenant Thrasher sent a message to them by one of the Albanian Partisans. The British relayed a radio message to the American forces in Italy, and the Americans sent a plane to drop supplies to the nurses and corpsmen. There were K rations and long winter underwear and GI shoes. These were welcome; but, as Agnes Jensen said later, no one had measured the nurses for size. The underwear had to be rolled up at the wrists and ankles. Ann Kopcso, a very small woman, had to wear six pairs of socks to make her shoes fit. Even so, they were much better than no shoes at all.

Once plans were made, through the British Secret Service radio, for planes to rescue the entire party, a small landing field was picked out and the Americans hid on a nearby hill. At exactly the prearranged time the planes came over: three transports, thirty-six fighter planes, even a bomber. Later Agnes Jensen wrote, "It was the prettiest

airshow I've seen, ever! I was absolutely amazed the army air force would put out all that equipment for so few of us."

Even so, the rescue was not successful. Because German forces were so close, the Americans on the ground could never give the proper signal for the planes to land. They could only stay hidden among the rocks and watch the planes circle and circle, until finally they flew away.

It was one of the corpsmen who said, "Well, if the army thinks that much of us, to send all those planes just for us, now we've got to get out."

By now one of the British Secret Service officers had joined the party. "If we can reach a certain spot on the coast," he told them, "British ships will pick us up."

So began another march. Agnes Jensen later wrote:

The day after Thanksgiving we crossed a mountain rather than go around it because German troops had moved into a town along the regular route. We learned later the Albanians never crossed that peak after September.

At almost the top of the mountain an enormous and ugly cloud moved in on us and we were suddenly in a severe blizzard. I had been in blizzards in northern Minnesota as a youngster, and would say this compared very well. The guides realized our trail was being covered by snow and they tried to race ahead. Our long line of followers began slipping, falling, and getting out of sight. I could not call to the person a few feet ahead, nor could I buck the wind enough to catch up.

Finally one of our sergeants came past me. I grabbed his arm but had to put my mouth right up to his ear to be heard. The wind was howling and snow was swirling with deafening noise. I told the sergeant to go ahead and hold up the guides until the rest of us could catch up.

Then, somehow, we just seemed to walk right out of the storm. We stumbled down the mountain to a little village below. The natives all seemed excited to see us and our interpreter told us they were calling us "Albanian heroes" because we had crossed their second highest mountain after *September.*

We could understand their excitement with no difficulty.

The coast was still a long way ahead. Because the Germans were so close there was one final, nonstop march of twenty-six hours. Agnes Jensen later said:

We made it to the coast the morning of January 8, exactly two months after our crash landing. I rolled over the crest about 9 A.M. My knees absolutely would not hold me any longer and I had to sit and slide down or risk falling with every step. But that Adriatic Sea really looked beautiful! A British ship picked us up about midnight and we arrived in Bari on the 9th, two months late.

And what of the three nurses who had disappeared, Lieutenants Lytle, Maness, and Porter? There was still no word.

✠

When the Germans attacked the village in which the Americans were hiding, Wilma Lytle, Ann Maness, and Helen Porter had been staying together in an Albanian home. Their host had told them not to run for the hills, but to hide in the cellar. The Germans, however, did not simply pass through the town after the fight with the Partisans. Instead, they made camp—directly across the street from the house where the nurses were hiding.

Days passed, then weeks, and the Germans were still there. They must have suspected that some of the Americans were still in the village, because time after time they searched the houses. The Albanians, however, had dug a tunnel from the house in which the nurses were staying to the one next door. When the Germans came, the nurses slipped through the tunnel into the next house. When the second house was searched, they slipped back to the first.

Weeks dragged on into months. The girls heard

through the underground grapevine that their friends had escaped. However, when they asked to be taken to the coast, they were told this was impossible. At last, in desperation, the nurses decided simply to start walking on their own. At this point one of the Albanians brought a small car to the back door of the house where the nurses were staying. In it, disguised as Albanian girls, they were slipped past the German troops. Later they were turned over to Secret Service men who helped them reach the coast. And at long last, on March 22, 1944, they rejoined their friends in Italy.

The trip that should have taken two hours had taken four and one-half months.

The official history of the army's Medical Department included a fitting summary of the adventure:

The performance of these nurses through the long weeks of their ordeal does indeed illumine a chapter of war which in the telling could have been another account of sordidness and suffering. They were involved in this situation because they had voluntarily gone to aid the sick and wounded in battle; by their performance among the natives, they won the friendship and strengthened the favorable reaction of the Albanians to the Allies; among themselves, the strong helped the sick through hardships; and when finally they were rescued they were ready not for publicity but simply to return to duty.

FRANCE AND GERMANY
CHAPTER TEN

By the spring of 1944 England was crowded with soldiers, American and British, French and Australian. English harbors were jammed with ships. Everyone was sure the Allies were about to invade German-occupied France. Medical units were alerted to be ready to move on a moment's notice—and then left waiting for days.

The question was: When would the invasion actually begin?

All during the night of June 5–6, Marjorie Peto heard planes passing overhead. But the 2nd General Hospital (where she was still Chief Nurse) was close to an airfield, and planes were always passing. Then in the morning she turned on her radio—and the calm voice of the British announcer was saying that the invasion had begun.

Paratroops were already fighting in France; gliders were bringing in more soldiers; men were landing on the beaches of Normandy. Casualties were heavy.

The fighting had scarcely moved inland from the beaches before the mobile field hospitals and evacuation hospitals followed. In England the nurses piled into trucks, wearing their combat uniforms: khaki jackets and shirts, baggy trousers and leggings, and high-topped shoes. They were loaded down with rain coats and helmets, musette bags and gas masks and canteens. "If some of us didn't have hair sticking out from under our helmets," one woman said, "nobody could tell us from the men."

From the trucks the nurses went on board ships. There were so many ships, coming and going, that the English Channel seemed to be an almost solid mass of them. Off the coast of France the nurses transferred to small boats, often the same landing craft the soldiers had been using hours before. On shore they set up their hospitals, in cow pastures, open fields, alongside the roads. The fighting was

only a few miles ahead and they could hear the guns booming. Overhead, Allied and German planes swirled in combat. Once a German plane crashed so close to a field hospital that fragments from it flew among the tents.

✠

In France the small, mobile field and evacuation hospitals leapfrogged past one another to keep up with the fighting. A hospital would be set up in tents or abandoned buildings, any shelter that had not been smashed by artillery. Casualties would pour in. Then as the fighting moved forward, a second hospital would bypass the first one and set up even closer to the front. Now the first hospital could finish giving emergency treatment to its patients and send them all to larger hospitals in the rear. Then would come its turn to leapfrog past the second hospital, following the battlefront.

As a result the nurses in the field hospitals lived largely in tents and close to the front. When it came time to move they rode in their own ambulances or in open trucks.

Often they would be jammed in with tremendous convoys carrying ammunition and food to the soldiers. Progress was slow. Sometimes it took all day to travel only a few miles. Sometimes the drivers became lost and might travel—or so it seemed to the girls—across half of France trying to find the next village. A medical unit on the move might spend its nights in open fields, without even tents.

It was on one such occasion that Lieutenant Caroline Renski was sitting beside the road with a group of other nurses. They were all in combat uniforms. There had been no chance to bathe or wash their clothes for several days. Some of the women sprawled on the ground asleep.

Others watched trucks loaded with troops moving toward the front.

Quite unconscious of what she was doing, Lieutenant Renski took off her helmet and ran her fingers through her blonde hair. Then she opened the battered, mud-stained musette bag she was carrying and searched through it until she found a wrinkled lavender hair ribbon. Casually she tied it in her bright hair. And from the passing trucks a great cheer went up. Many of the men going into battle would take with them the memory of the pretty woman in filthy combat clothing, and the lavender ribbon in her blonde hair.

Almost without exception the American soldiers had tremendous respect for their nurses. Wounded men often wrote letters expressing appreciation for what had been done for them. It was in reply to these that Lieutenant Frances Slanger wrote one of the most touching letters to come out of the war. It read:

It is 0200 [2 A.M.] and I have been lying awake for one hour listening to the steady, even breathing of the other three nurses in the tent and thinking of some of the things we had discussed during the day. The rain is beating down on the tent with torrential force. The wind is on a mad rampage....

The fire is burning low and just a few live coals are on the bottom.... I couldn't help thinking how similar to a human being a fire is. If it is not allowed to run down too low, and if there is a spark of life left in it, it can be nursed back—and so can a human being. It's slow, it's gradual, it's done all the time in these field hospitals....

We had read several articles in different magazines and papers sent in by grateful GIs praising the work of nurses around the combat areas. Praising us—for what?

...The GIs say we rough it. We in our little tent can't see it. True, we are set up in tents, sleep on cots and are subject to the temperament of the weather. We wade ankle deep in mud, but you have to lie in it.... You, the men behind the guns, the men driving our tanks, flying our planes, sailing our ships...it's to you we doff our helmets. To every GI wearing the

American uniform, for you we have the greatest admiration.

Yes, this time we are handing out the bouquets. After taking care of some of your buddies, seeing them when they are brought in bloody, dirty with earth, mud and grime...seeing them gradually brought back to life and consciousness, to see their lips separate into a grin when they first welcome you! It doesn't amaze us to hear one of them say, "Hiya, Babe," or "Holy mackerel, an American woman!"

...Rough it? No! It is a privilege to be able to receive you and it is a great distinction to see you open your eyes and with that swell American grin say, "Hiya, Babe!"

After writing this letter Frances Slanger showed it to her tent mates. They all signed it and sent it to the *Stars and Stripes*, the army newspaper. The paper printed it, and from all over the world GIs wrote in answer. One of the letters, printed in the *Stars and Stripes*, said:

We men were not given the choice of working on the battlefield or the home front.... We are here because we have to be. You are here merely because you felt you were needed.... You could be home, soaking yourselves in a bathtub every day, putting on clean clothes over a clean body and crawling in between clean sheets at night. Instead, you endure whatever hardships you must to be where you can do us the most good.

I'd better stop now, because I am getting sentimental, but I want you to know your "editorial" did not change but only confirmed my deep respect for you modern Florence Nightingales. If the world had a few more people like you in it, there wouldn't be any wars.

Frances Slanger never had a chance to see her letter in print nor any of the answers. She had written it before dawn on October 21, 1944. Later that same day, off duty, she returned to her tent to wrap Christmas presents in time to mail them to her family. A German shell struck the tent. A half-hour later Lieutenant Slanger, Army Nurse Corps, was dead. Many a GI, however, would remember her letter, and before the war was over a hospital ship would be named in her honor.

That Christmas of 1944 was one that a great many nurses, especially those in the European theater, would remember for a long time. By mid-December, Allied troops had fought their way through France and into Germany. It looked as if the war would soon be over. Then the German army launched one last desperate offensive in what came to be known as the Battle of the Bulge.

Bernice Tansy—the older nurse who had had so much trouble drilling other nurses in training camp—was stationed with the 140th General Hospital in southeastern Belgium. The hospital was in what had once been a Catholic school, surrounded by wide lawns. The fighting had moved far enough away so that the hospital seemed quiet and peaceful. As Christmas approached, Lieutenant Tansy and the other nurses prepared to make it a cheerful time for their patients.

All over the world military hospitals were preparing for Christmas. In the South Pacific the Christmas tree might have to be made from palm fronds. In the Aleutians it might be only a scrubby and almost leafless bush cut from some barren hillside. In the jungles of New Guinea, corpsmen cut stars from empty gasoline tins, and nurses made Christmas tree ornaments from jungle flowers and scraps of colored parachute silk. Navy tradition required every ship to have a Christmas tree tied to its mast, and the hospital ships followed this tradition, though sometimes the tree was strange indeed.

For Bernice Tansy and the nurses of the 140th General, there were only minor difficulties. Trees were set up in all the wards. Nurses and corpsmen wrapped small presents, making sure that every patient would have some gift.

Then one morning Miss Tansy awoke to hear the sound of guns. They were big guns, a long way off; but she had not heard guns for some time and she wondered about them. During the day German planes appeared more and more often. Allied planes tangled with them in dogfights, and off-duty nurses, standing on the hospital lawn, could see the white vapor trails of the swirling planes high overhead.

Abruptly the hospital received orders to evacuate all the patients who could be moved. Long lines of ambulances streamed onto the grounds, loaded, and departed.

Next day new patients began to arrive. These were battle casualties, fresh from the front. With them came stories of the German offensive. German troops had broken through the American lines. Tanks and armored cars were pouring through. German planes were dropping paratroopers behind the American lines. Some of the Germans were wearing American uniforms, and you could no longer be sure who was friend and who was foe. Guards appeared around the hospital, and anyone going in or out had to use a password.

There was no time now to think about Christmas. The nurses worked twelve hours on and twelve hours off, around the clock.

Then came orders to evacuate the hospital, immediately. German troops were only a few miles away and might reach the area at any time.

Once more the wounded were loaded into ambulances and sent to other hospitals in the rear. The medical personnel followed, some jammed into ambulances, some in open trucks. Bernice Tansy and the other nurses were allowed to take only what they could carry with them. Christmas presents were left unopened and clothing left hanging in closets. In the confusion some of the nurses reached one rear hospital, some another. Wherever they went they found work to be done.

Perhaps no nurse in the army had a more confusing Christmas that year than Lieutenant Sally Zumaris of East Moline, Illinois. Her hospital was set up in what, before the war, had been a nobleman's chateau. She had written home about it:

There are about 100 rooms. Our operating room is located in what was formerly the ballroom. It has lovely drapes, mirrors, rose-satin brocaded walls, the most beautiful chandeliers, and hardwood floors. Can you imagine me waltzing from patient to patient? ...My blue room, which I share with five other nurses, contains needlepoint-covered chairs, rugs, beautiful inlaid bedside tables, wardrobe, mirrors, electric lights, and, for contrast, six army canvas cots....

We had a party here before we received any patients. The Baron, the Baroness, their two daughters and son came.... The son played the grand piano and I watched with the Baron.

Nine days before Christmas, in the period of comparative calm that preceded the Battle of the Bulge, Sally and two other nurses were given leave to visit Paris. They were there, and having a wonderful time, when the news of the great German breakthrough reached them. Immediately the girls jumped in their jeep and headed back for the hospital, knowing they would be needed.

It was not easy going. The roads were jammed with troops and supplies moving toward the front, empty trucks and wounded going to the rear. At night there was a total blackout. Guards were everywhere, looking for any German paratroopers who had been dropped behind the lines. The girls took turns driving, day and night. Later Sally wrote to a friend:

After accidentally bumping into a gasoline dump near the front and a few other mishaps of blackout driving, we finally arrived in Ettelbruck, only to see artillery shooting in the direction of the hospital. I don't know why, but the M.P.s let us go through. As we dashed into the building we found it was deserted—no one answered our call of "Is anybody home?" The floors and hallways were littered with paper, boxes, etc., only our beautifully decorated Christmas trees were intact. They seemed so strange standing there in the dim light....

Suddenly artillery fire was overhead again. We three plunked our helmets on our heads and ran up to the third floor.... We wanted to see if any of our personal belongings were left in our rooms.

Upstairs, they ran into a sight that stopped them in their tracks, terrified. The third floor was filled with soldiers. But they were American soldiers, as surprised as the nurses at the meeting.

The hospital, the soldiers said, had moved three days before. So once more the nurses took to their jeep. "And what a ride that was!" Sally wrote to her friend. "All along the front lines. Jerry planes were overhead, antiaircraft firing, M.P.s stopping us, asking for the password, and how surprised they'd be when they heard my faltering feminine voice."

At last they reached a hospital. It was not their own unit, but it did not matter now. There were new casualties to care for.

✚

Gradually, in bitter fighting, the German offensive was blunted and then turned back. Once more Allied troops moved forward, the medical units close behind them. Bernice Tansy and the 140th General returned to find the Catholic school building in which their hospital had been located still intact. The Christmas trees were still standing, the presents unwrapped. Everything was just as they had left it, or almost. One German armored car had reached the hospital gate—and run out of gas. One German paratrooper had come down on the wide lawn—but something had gone wrong with his landing and his neck had been broken by the fall.

War had created a tragic Christmas for both sides.

PRISONERS OF WAR
CHAPTER ELEVEN

At Christmastime in 1944, Ruth Stoltz and her friend Minnie Breese were confined in the Santo Tomas internment camp in Manila, the largest city of the Philippine Islands. Like other nurses captured in the tunnels of Corregidor, they had been prisoners of the Japanese for two and a half years.

The prisoners had little idea of what was going on in the outside world. Their guards claimed that Japan was winning the war. The nurses did not believe this. They did not dare believe it. They lived on hope, and as months dragged into years it began to seem as if hope were all they might have to live on.

At first it had not been so bad, except for the crowding. The internment camp was located in what had once been the Royal and Pontifical University of Santo Tomas. There were big, old-fashioned buildings spread over a campus of sixty-five acres and surrounded by a high iron fence. Inside this fence the prisoners could move about as they pleased. But most of the buildings had been intended for classrooms and offices, not for living quarters, and certainly not for 3,000 or 4,000 people. The nurses slept crowded together in a few small rooms. Each nurse was given one cot—that was all. Between the cots there was barely space to move. Whatever belongings the women had managed to bring with them had to go on the floor beneath the cots.

These cots were made of a kind of woven bamboo, like the seat of a porch chair. At first there were not even mattresses. And when some of the nurses were given bed-pads, they had to get rid of them. "The trouble was," Ruth Stoltz explained later, "that living jammed up together like that, in those old, old buildings, there were bedbugs. By the thousands. We couldn't get them out of the mattresses. But we could take the cots outside every few days and pour boiling water over them to kill the bugs. Also, the cots were cool. We learned to sleep on them quite comfortably."

The nurses were the only military personnel the Japanese allowed in this camp. All the other prisoners were American and British civilians, men, women, and children who had been living in the Philippines when the war began. The hospital was set up in what had been a girls' dormitory. Many of the patients were old; some were children. But at first there was no great crowding, and the nurses were not overworked. Indeed, the nurses were glad to have work, something to help them pass the long, dreary hours and keep them from thinking too much about the future.

The food was not good but, in the early days, it was fairly plentiful. The Japanese fed the prisoners fish and rice chiefly. But there were also Red Cross supplies, and each day Filipinos would come to the high iron fence to sell fresh fruits and vegetables. Some of the prisoners still had a little money left.

The prisoners were allowed to run their own camp, under Japanese supervision. Conditions here were far, far better than in the prisoner-of-war camps where the captured soldiers had been sent.

Then, gradually, things began to change. Where three meals had been served each day in the camp, now there

were only two—at morning and at night. The nurses lined up with the other prisoners, each carrying a mess kit and a meal ticket. The ticket was punched at each meal so that no one could come back for more. Also, the Red Cross packages became scarce, and the Filipinos at the high iron fence had less to sell. Ruth Stoltz told her friend Minnie, "I wish now I were fat. This would be a fine time to reduce."

"It looks as if we all are going to reduce," Minnie said, "whether we want to or not."

For a long while most of the conversation in the camp had been about the war. Since no one knew anything for sure there were always rumors: The Japanese fleet had been wiped out.... The American fleet had been wiped out.... The Japanese had captured Hawaii.... General MacArthur was about to invade the Philippines....

But as time went on the talk became more and more about food. The hungry nurses sat in their small crowded rooms and told one another what they were going to eat when at last the war was over and they got home. They were going to eat steaks by the dozen and drink milk by the gallon. They were going to eat peanut butter sandwiches topped with whipped cream. They were going to eat great mounds of potatoes floating in melted butter.

Once a few potatoes were brought into the camp; nobody seemed quite sure how they got there. The nurses made certain that the potatoes were served to the old, to the very sick, and to the children. Some of the young children could not remember how a potato tasted—and did not like them.

Many of the nurses and other prisoners planted gardens. But with no fertilizer and no tools the gardens did not grow well.

But the prisoners had a quality that their Japanese captors did not seem to understand: The British and Americans kept their sense of humor. From the first the Japanese had demanded that, whenever a prisoner passed a Japanese army officer, the prisoner must stop and bow. Anyone who did not would be punished, perhaps beaten. So the Americans bowed, and made jokes about it.

One day Ruth and Minnie were leaving the hospital when they saw a Japanese officer approaching. Ruth looked at her friend, grinning. "Do you have your curtsy all ready?"

"I'd like to drop him a curtsy," Minnie said. "Right on his flat head."

Both nurses laughed, and the officer approached them angrily. He spoke English, and for ten minutes he lectured them on manners. "You do not behave properly," he told them. "You are a conquered people. Your nation has been defeated. You have lost face. Yet you do not show proper respect for your conquerors. You have no right to laugh. Only a people with no self-respect can laugh at defeat."

The girls listened to him. When he was finished they bowed politely. The officer walked away. Then the nurses looked at each other and broke into howls of laughter. For they did not believe they were defeated; nor would they ever be defeated so long as they kept the ability to laugh at adversity.

Even so, life in the prison went from bad to worse. Food became even more scarce. The iron fence through which the Filipinos had sold fruits and vegetables was made into a solid wall by the Japanese. Now even those prisoners who still had money could not buy food.

Japanese soldiers began to search the camp more and more often. They were looking, they said, for weapons, but it was money they were after chiefly. Now all prisoners were ordered to turn over any money they had to the Japanese. Anyone who did not would be severely punished. Ruth Stoltz, who still had a few American dollars, kept them hidden in a ball of yarn. Often the Japanese would pick up the yarn, look at it, and put it down again. But they never found the money.

By the fall of 1944, as the third year of imprisonment continued, the conditions in the camp were growing desperate. Food consisted mostly of mush—more hot water than corn meal. Sometimes there was soybean soup and a little rice. Everyone in the camp now was thin, gaunt. The hospital began to fill up, particularly with elderly people. The nurses and the civilian doctors did their best, but there was very little medicine. Besides, most of the patients needed food more than medicine.

Then, on September 21, 1944, came a cheering episode.

Ruth Stoltz was in the hospital when she heard the sound of guns. She had heard them often enough on Corregidor to recognize that sound. But what could the Japanese be shooting at? She ran outside to look.

Off to the east the sky was speckled with the small

black clouds of antiaircraft fire. As Ruth watched, there came the sound of motors, growing louder, turning into a roar as an airplane flashed overhead, followed by another, and another and another—blue-gray planes with the white star of the United States painted on their wings! As they passed overhead, the pilots—who knew the location of the internment camp, wiggled their wings in greeting. And on the ground the nurses cheered until they were hoarse. They pounded one another on the back and laughed and cried together. If American planes could attack Manila, surely the day of liberation must be near.

One raid, however, did not mean the end of the war. Instead there were more and more restrictions from the Japanese. In December, four of the prisoners who had acted as camp directors were taken away and killed without any explanation. The food ration became still more scanty. By January the men in Santo Tomas had lost an average of fifty-one pounds each; the women had lost an average of thirty-two pounds. In the hospital the death rate increased sharply. The Japanese ordered the American doctors not to put the word "Starvation" on the death certificate but to give some other reason. When the doctors refused, the chief doctor was arrested.

By the end of January everyone in the camp knew that rescue must come soon, or it would be too late.

In the early evening of February 3, 1945, Ruth Stoltz and another nurse sat on a cot playing double solitaire. They were thin. Even in the pale light their cheek bones and collarbones showed against the skin. Somewhere to the north there was the sound of gunfire, but there had been gunfire for several days now. There had been so many disappointments in the past that they dared not hope too much.

Still, the gunfire did sound closer than ever before.

"Maybe..." Ruth said. But the firing had stopped, and the other nurse merely shook her head.

Outside the building someone shouted, "Americans! Americans!"

The girls leaped up. Running to the window, they knocked cots over in their excitement.

An armored tank was coming through the camp gate and up the driveway. But whose tank? No one could be sure.

Fifty yards away the tank stopped. The top opened and the head and shoulders of a man appeared. And still in the half-darkness no one could be sure.

Then the man shouted. No one knew what he was shouting at, but they could hear his voice. And leaning far out of the window Ruth said to her friend, "That's an American all right!"

After that it was chaos. From all the buildings people were running, shouting, laughing, crying. They hugged one another. They hugged the soldiers who followed the tank. They staggered from weakness, and danced with joy.

Later a reporter would ask Ruth Stoltz how she had felt at this moment. She could only look at him and smile. "I can't tell you," she said. "Because there are no words for that sort of thing. There are just no words."

The liberation of Santo Tomas and the other prison

camps in the Philippines did not mark the final end of the war. The great invasion of Okinawa was still to come; the bombs were still to fall on the Japanese cities of Hiroshima and Nagasaki. But for most of the nurses who had been Japanese prisoners—those who had served the longest and suffered the most—the war was over. And for the others the end was in sight.

When at long last the war was over, most of the nurses returned to civilian life. Some, like Edith Vowell and Ruth Stoltz, stayed in the service to become majors and lieutenant colonels.

To all of them—these heroic women who had voluntarily endangered themselves to heal broken bodies and broken spirits as well—the entire nation would owe an eternal debt of gratitude.

AUTHOR'S NOTE

Not very much has been written about the American military nurses who served with such courage and endurance and devotion to duty in World War II. Consequently, in researching this book I often had to rely on personal contact with nurses who could tell me about their experiences. I want to say thanks to all of them who have been so extremely generous with their help. They have scrambled through attics and dug into bureau drawers to uncover scrapbooks and memories. Quite literally, without their help this book could not have been written.

I especially want to say thanks to: Mrs. George Clemens, for permission to quote from letters written by her friend Phyllis MacDonald Smith; to Dorothy Kenton Deere, Wilma Lytle Gibson, Martha Halfpenny Howard, Leota Hurley Leavens, Agnes Jensen Magerich, Janice Feagin Olson, Marie Pirl Smith, Ruth Stolz, Bernice Tansy, and Edith Vowell. (If some of the names used here are longer than those used in the book it is because marriages have made additions. In the book itself I have used the nurses' maiden names.)

I would also like to say thanks to the officers and people of the Magazine and Book Branch of the Department of Defense's Directorate of Information Service, and to the Historical Unit of the U.S. Army Medical Service. I don't know them personally, but somebody there has put in a lot of time looking up information for me.

Many, many thanks.

WYATT BLASSINGAME
1967

About the Author

Wyatt Blassingame wrote 600 magazine articles and short stories, five adult novels, and almost 60 books for young readers over a writing career that lasted longer than a half-century. A keen and curious observer of life and natural history, he wrote about the egrets, raccoons, crows, and other creatures that showed up in his backyard on the island of Anna Maria, Florida. He studied and wrote about sharks, snakes, turtles, armadillos, and even wrote a book on *The Little Killers: Fleas, Ticks, Mosquitos*. While everything interested him, he became known as a Florida writer, as many of his novels and stories were set there.

Born in Alabama, Wyatt graduated from the University of Alabama in 1929. Wyatt had many adventures as a young man. During the Great Depression, he earned the nickname "Hobo" for his skill at jumping trains and hitchhiking across the country to find work. He was a police reporter and taught college journalism before moving to New York City where he began writing mystery and detective stories for the "pulp" magazines, earning a penny a word. In one year, he pounded out 500 stories on his Underwood typewriter. He enlisted at the outbreak of World War II and served in the Navy in the Pacific, earning a Bronze Star. His experiences led him later to write about those he saw as true heroes and heroines, those who served on the medical front.

In 1936, he married Gertie Olsen and moved to Anna Maria Island, Florida, an idyllic slice of white sand in the Gulf of Mexico, where they raised two daughters. Wyatt continued writing until his death in 1985, filling his free time with fishing, swimming, and gardening. He kept nature notes of the Island's weather, tides, plants, and animals, and for his novels, he researched the Florida cattle industry, the real estate boom of the 1920s, and the history and culture of the Seminoles. In 1952, he was asked to write a book for young readers about a subject dear to his heart: *The Great Trains of the World*. That book was followed by dozens more, including *Frogmen in World War II, The French Foreign Legion, The Incas and the Spanish Conquest,* and *The Look-It-Up Book of Presidents*, which has remained in print, updated every four years. He wrote biographies of Eleanor Roosevelt, Sacagawea, and Thor Heyerdahl, among others. Wyatt also published a series of Tall Tales about mythic and legendary characters, like Paul Bunyan and Pecos Bill.

Wyatt Blassingame was a man with foresight and compassion. He and his wife were early advocates for the environment, ahead of their time. They served on Anna Maria's city planning and zoning boards, and both fought to prevent opening Tampa Bay to oil exploration. Wyatt was also an early defender of civil rights. His prize-winning story, "Man's Courage," dealt with racial hatred in the army, and won the Ben Franklin Award for the Best Short Story of 1956.

With his bushy eyebrows and deep southern drawl, Wyatt Blassingame was respected by his friends and circle of fellow writers, and beloved by his family. His daughter Peggy gave him five grandchildren and ten great-grandchildren, and his daughter April's four children blessed him with nine more grandchildren, all of whom will be able to read this story again in print, thanks to Purple House Press. The family and descendants of Wyatt Blassingame are happy and grateful that his work is available to a new generation.

KATHI DIAMANT
Granddaughter of Wyatt Blassingame
October 2021

www.ingramcontent.com/pod-product-compliance
Lightning Source LLC
Chambersburg PA
CBHW030333100526
44592CB00010B/678